Nicky J Davies

THE CORPORATE SUCCESS PATHWAY

Proven strategies for
coaches, consultants and
trainers to consistently
win corporate clients

Rethink

First published in Great Britain in 2025
by Rethink Press (www.rethinkpress.com)

Contents

Introduction

A s coaches, consultants and trainers, we're in this work because we care about helping people grow, develop and transform. We're driven by a desire to do meaningful work, to contribute to others' success and to see the impact of our skills in the world, but if you want to expand that impact beyond individuals and small businesses, working with corporate clients opens up a different level of opportunity. It's a way to achieve more consistency in your business, command higher fees and work on initiatives that reach people across entire teams, departments and organisations.

Corporate clients aren't just big-name private companies. They include government agencies, public services, medium and large businesses, and not-for-profits such as schools, universities and chari-ties. I define the corporate sector as any organisation with around 500 employees or more. Why? Because these organisations have structures, systems and peo-ple dynamics that create consistent demand for exter-nal expertise. They have budgets to invest, people challenges to solve and the infrastructure to imple-ment meaningful change, making them an ideal fit for the kind of work you and I do.

Shifting your focus towards corporate clients doesn't mean abandoning the clients you've worked with up until now. You've already built a strong business help-ing individuals and small businesses, and that work can continue to thrive. By adding more corporate cli-ents into the mix, you open the door to longer-term engagements, more strategic projects and a business model that delivers higher rewards for your time and energy. The corporate world offers you the chance to increase your revenue while reducing the constant hustle of chasing smaller, one-off clients. You move towards a business that feels calmer, more predictable and more impactful.

Perhaps you've already had a taste of corporate work – a couple of workshops, a one-off big project, enough to know the opportunity is real – but it's felt inconsistent or difficult to repeat. Maybe you've seen others landing multiple contracts or becoming trusted advisors to leadership teams and wondered, *How do I make that my norm?*

It's not about questioning your ability. You already know you do great work. It's about turning occasional wins into something more consistent, a predictable and reliable part of your business. That's exactly where this book comes in.

I get it, I've been through this too. Like you, I'm a coach, consultant and trainer. I've spent years investing in my skills, qualifications and personal development because I care about doing great work. I started my business serving individuals and small business owners and enjoyed the work, but I also felt the limits of that model. There's only so much you can do working with individuals before you run into time constraints or burnout. I realised early on that corporate clients didn't just offer bigger budgets – they gave me the chance to work on more meaningful, larger projects that had ripple effects across organisations.

Since I started my business in 2004, I've worked with more than 130 organisations in twenty-eight countries, including well-known brands like Vodafone, Maersk, G4S, the National Health Service (NHS) and ENGIE. Many of my corporate clients have stayed with me for over a decade, some for as long as fourteen years. Through these long-term relationships, I've been able to deepen my impact, create predictable revenue and build a business that feels fulfilling rather than frantic.

I haven't just experienced this shift myself. I've helped other coaches, consultants and trainers do the same. You'll hear their stories throughout this book. The Corporate Success Pathway I'll be sharing with you is the distillation of everything I've learned about winning and retaining corporate clients. It's a practical, proven approach that helps you build genuine relationships with decision makers and turn sporadic corporate work into a stable, high-value part of your business.

I know what it's like to feel unsure about how to take the next step. Even with experience and expertise it can feel unclear how to position yourself in the corporate space, especially when the world of organisations seems complex or opaque from the outside. I remember coming out of the public sector with no sales experience and no idea how to connect with corporate decision makers. I had to learn it piece by piece, through trial, error and persistence.

You might be in a similar position, successful in your own right but feeling that reaching corporate decision makers is somehow harder. You may be wondering, *How do I position what I do in a way that resonates with corporates? How do I build credibility without years of a corporate background? How do I get in front of decision makers without feeling like I'm selling? How do I land bigger projects without losing what I love about my business?*

These are the questions this book is designed to answer. You don't need to become someone you're not. You don't need to overhaul your business. You already have deep expertise and a track record of delivering value to clients. This book is about helping you take what you've already built and expand it into the corporate space in a way that feels aligned, authentic and sustainable.

The game has changed

If it feels like there are more coaches, consultants and trainers than ever before, you're right, there are. On top of that, the world we're working in has shifted and the ways in which we used to attract and win clients don't work as well anymore. What once felt straightforward – building relationships, securing referrals and growing by word of mouth – now feels slower, noisier and harder to cut through.

You might have noticed it yourself. If you've found it harder to stand out lately and open new doors with corporate clients, it's not your imagination. The coaching, consulting and training world has grown massively over the last decade, and with it, the landscape has changed. By understanding the shifts, you can adjust your approach and create the kind of stability, impact and freedom you were aiming for when you first set out on your business journey.

Take coaching, for example. Back in 2015, there were around 53,000 coach practitioners globally.[1] Fast-forward to 2023, and that number has doubled to over 100,000. Revenue produced by coaches has grown too, climbing by 63% between 2015 and 2022, and it's on track to reach US$7.3 billion globally by the end of 2025.[2] That's a huge amount of growth in a relatively short time.

Consulting has expanded globally as well, moving from a US$1 trillion market in 2015 to nearly US$1.8 trillion in 2023.[3] Even with a contraction in 2024, markets like the UK are rebounding, driven by investment in technology and AI.[4]

On the training side, companies continue to invest heavily in their people. Organisations now spend an average of US$1,300 per employee each year on professional development, with even more allocated for leadership development and executive coaching.[5]

In my experience, corporates don't hesitate to invest when they find the right partner. We regularly deliver coaching and training solutions worth between £50,000 and £78,000. Our consulting contracts are worth even more. What all of this tells us is that corporates are continuing to invest in these services, and they're investing big, but they're looking for trusted experts who can demonstrate real impact. The demand is there – the market for coaching, consulting and training is bigger and noisier than ever – but what's harder is cutting through the noise. Old tactics like relying solely on referrals or posting general content on LinkedIn are not enough anymore.

Success in this space isn't about being the loudest voice. It's about being the most relevant by showing you understand your potential client's world, their challenges and the outcomes that matter to them. When you align your approach with how corporates buy today, you unlock more consistent opportunities and greater freedom and make a deeper impact.

This book is here to help you do exactly that.

Building a consistent flow of corporate clients

The Corporate Success Pathway is a practical, repeatable approach designed for experienced coaches, consultants and trainers who want to move beyond one-off projects and build a steady, consistent flow of corporate clients. It gives you the structure and confidence to create high-trust relationships with organisations that genuinely value your expertise, and will lead to longer-term, higher-value opportunities. The five steps of Position, Package, Price, Prospect and Promote I explain in Part Two are drawn from what works in the real world. They reflect how corporate decisions are made, how trust is built over time and how you can show up in ways that open doors, not just once, but again and again, to become a trusted partner. This is the goal: not just to land a gig or two, but to build something sustainable.

I know the struggle of constantly reinventing your services, trying to price your offers without second-guessing yourself, and spending time promoting your work without seeing traction. I also know the doubts that creep in: *Do they really need what I offer? Will they take me seriously on my own? Is it even worth the effort?*

Yes, they do. Yes, they will. Yes, it is – but only if you're doing the right things, in the right order, with the right approach.

Let's walk through what that looks like.

1. We start with **Position**. This is where we get crystal clear on the problems you solve for organisations and how you want to be known. You'll learn how to identify your niche using the WPO model: who you help, the problems you solve and the outcomes you deliver. This ensures your messaging is sharp, relevant and immediately appealing to corporate decision makers.

2. Next comes **Package**. Here, we ensure your services are structured in ways that make corporates eager to buy. You'll learn how to shape your expertise into offers that give quick wins, as well as addressing more substantial issues like team or leadership development, culture and transformational change. The key is making sure your offers speak directly to

the challenges corporate leaders are grappling with and the kinds of outcomes they care about. Together we'll shape your services into clear, compelling offers that demonstrate value, relevance and impact so it's easier for corporate decision makers to say yes.

3. Then we come to **Price.** This is where many experienced practitioners hold themselves back. In this step, you'll learn how to price confidently, knowing and stating the value you deliver at an organisational level. You'll move past undercharging and second-guessing into setting fees that reflect the value of your work and the outcomes you generate.

4. Next, we turn to **Prospect** and identifying the right decision makers in organisations that are a good fit for your work. This is about being focused and knowing where to look and who to connect with to make that first approach count.

5. Finally, we focus on **Promote**. We'll tackle this in a focused way that helps you become known and trusted in the right circles. Corporates recognise they need external expertise and regularly invest in services like yours, but they don't want to feel like they're being sold to. Decision makers are constantly approached with sales pitches, so what they respond to is a different kind of interaction – one where the conversation is useful and relevant to them from the outset. When you shift from selling to offering value and insights,

you create the kind of engagement that leads naturally to paid opportunities without the awkwardness of a hard sell. That's why we'll focus on how to spark meaningful conversations that offer real value to decision makers from the start. We'll cover practical, low-pressure strategies like insight interviews and curating round-table discussions that corporate leaders genuinely want to be part of. It's about building long-term visibility and credibility without burning out or becoming glued to LinkedIn.

By us working through the five steps together, you'll find it much easier to get in front of the right decision makers, start meaningful conversations and open the doors to opportunities that fit well and position you as a trusted partner.

Becoming a trusted partner means you're not just hired to deliver a session or tick a box. You're invited into the room to help shape and create something bigger. You are part of conversations about how the organisation can navigate significant changes, develop its talented people, improve team effectiveness, strengthen its managers and leaders, and move towards its vision. It's no longer transactional. You are working alongside decision makers to co-create solutions that matter. You're helping them think things through and then deliver what's been agreed. That changes everything.

The five steps might seem simple on the surface but they are deeply strategic and carefully sequenced. They reflect how corporate buying decisions are made, what builds trust over time and how to stay visible and relevant without feeling you have to become someone you are not.

Throughout this book, you'll hear stories from coaches and consultants who've used the Corporate Success Pathway to shift their businesses towards more stability, revenue and freedom. You'll see how they moved from sporadic corporate work to consistent contracts, from small client bases to larger, more strategic partnerships, all while staying true to the work they love to do.

Building meaningful corporate relationships takes time, intention and consistency, but it's absolutely achievable when you follow a structured pathway that's designed around how corporate buying decisions are made. If you're here for quick wins, there are other books that will make bigger promises. If, however, you're here to build a business that feels simpler, more fulfilling and more financially stable while helping organisations thrive, this is the place for you.

The Corporate Success Pathway is different from generic marketing or sales models. It's built specifically for the unique dynamics of working with larger organisations. It's focused on relationship-driven selling, aligned offers and consistent positioning – things that lead to genuine partnerships and long-term success.

This book is your guide to building a business that moves from occasional corporate projects to consistent, high-value client relationships, creating a legacy of impact, influence and meaningful work. By the time you reach the end, you'll have the clarity, tools and confidence to make corporate work a natural, sustainable and enjoyable part of your business journey, amplifying the strengths you already have.

Let's get started.

PART ONE
TIME TO EVOLVE

B efore we get into the how, we need to pause and look at the why. Not just why corporates matter, but why what's worked for you up to now may not be enough for where you want to go next.

If you're reading this, you're likely an experienced coach, consultant or trainer. You've made an impact. You've seen people change, teams shift, leaders grow. Maybe you've worked with private clients and small businesses and had a few corporate projects come your way. If you're honest with yourself, however, there's probably still a gap between the impact you know you're capable of and the consistency you'd like in your business. You are not alone. Many skilled professionals are doing meaningful work yet still find themselves with a business that works but still feels too unpredictable. One month feels great, the next is quieter. Corporate opportunities come through from time to time, but it's not as steady or sustainable as you'd like. It's not because you're not good enough. You know you get results. It's because the dynamics shift when you step into the corporate world, and most people were never shown how to navigate that shift.

In this part of the book, we'll unpack what that shift looks like. We'll look at why working primarily with private clients or small businesses can quietly limit your growth and why some build steady, well-paid corporate relationships, while others, equally capable, never quite gain traction. We'll explore why visibility alone isn't enough to attract corporate opportunities, and we'll take an honest look at what's required to build trust and influence in a corporate context. We'll think about why now is the perfect time to work with corporate clients, and we'll finish this part by taking an honest look at the challenges of running a business in an uncertain climate so you can make conscious, confident decisions about the next stage of your business.

You've already built something meaningful and now it's about expanding it. This isn't about abandoning what makes your work powerful. It's about developing how you think, how you show up and how you're perceived so that you can create more impact, with more consistency, without compromising who you are. Now, more than ever, is the time to make this shift. Corporates are actively seeking fresh ideas, external support and solutions that work. They're ready, but they won't find you unless you learn how to show up in ways they recognise, respect and respond to.

This part is designed to challenge you. To surface the unconscious, outdated assumptions and habits that might be holding you back. More than that, it's designed to help you reconnect with your strengths, to see how much more is possible when you stop playing small and start approaching your business in a way that fits the world you want to work in – one that genuinely aligns with who you are and the life you want to lead.

You're not starting over – you are building on solid ground. Now it's time to evolve. Let's dive in.

1
Private Clients And Small Businesses Versus Corporate Clients

If you've built your business around private clients or small businesses, you'll know how rewarding it can be. There's something human about it. You get to work closely with people and see the difference you're making, and you often develop strong, personal relationships. Witnessing moments of transformation can be deeply fulfilling, but, if you're honest, you probably also know the flip side. The part that feels fragile, unpredictable and sometimes draining.

It doesn't matter how skilled you are, how much heart you bring or how many glowing testimonials you collect, there's a hard limit on how far this model can take you. Private individuals and small businesses often love what you do, but they rarely have the budget, scale or ongoing need to sustain a longer-term partnership. You help them, they are grateful, and then it ends. You find yourself back in motion again, filling the pipeline, chasing leads, wondering where the next 'yes' will come from. Even when things are going well, there's often a quiet sense that it could all shift in a moment.

I know that feeling well. In the early years of running my business, I leaned heavily on private clients and small business projects. It felt familiar and safe, even if the income wasn't. I had months when everything looked like it was working with a few retainers, a couple of short contracts and a handful of referrals. Then, seemingly overnight, it would go quiet with no warning. I'd be working just as hard, but the momentum would be gone and the uncertainty would creep back in.

It was exhausting, not just physically, but emotionally. That quiet fear of worrying, *Is this ever going to be stable?* lingered in the background, even during the good times. No matter how many hours I put in, the foundations never felt secure. What I came to realise was that I needed to build my business differently. That realisation was the beginning of everything shifting.

When I began focusing on larger clients, organisations with scale, structure and an appetite for long-term development, everything changed. I was no longer starting over every few months. I was building relationships, not just chasing contracts. The work still felt meaningful, but now it was also sustainable.

This is the path this book will take you on, but before we go further, it's worth taking a moment to be clear on the key differences between the worlds of private clients and small businesses, and the corporate space. That clarity is part of what helps you move forward with more confidence knowing you're not leaving behind what you love about your work but adding more stability and opportunity to it.

The benefits of change

Let's look first at what the private client model typically brings:

- **Inconsistent income**: You're often reliant on short-term projects or one-off sessions. Even your best months can't guarantee what's coming next.

- **Lower budgets**: Even when they value your work, most small businesses and individuals don't have the financial capacity to invest at the level that reflects your full value.

- **Time-for-money trap**: Your earnings are directly tied to your personal capacity. There's little room to scale unless you're constantly delivering.

- **No clear growth path**: Even if you love your clients, there's often nowhere for the relationship to go. You quickly hit a ceiling.

Now let's look at what becomes possible when you shift to corporate clients:

- **Predictable revenue**: Corporate clients often allocate annual budgets for coaching, consulting and training. This creates the potential for longer-term contracts, repeat business and financial stability you can plan around.

- **Scalability**: Your work can extend well beyond one-to-one delivery. You can work with cohorts, teams or entire departments. You can build programmes, licence content and create sustainable ways to increase your impact without increasing your hours.

- **Valuing your talent**: When corporate clients see the value, they're willing to invest. Executive coaching fees can range from £350 to £1,500 per session. Two-day workshops often land between £4,500 and £8,000. Leadership development programmes regularly run to £50,000–£100,000 for a single cohort. This isn't about inflating your fees, it's about matching your value to the level of investment corporates are already prepared to make.

The shift from primarily private clients and small businesses to corporates is about making the work you already love go further both for you and for the organisations you serve. When you learn to align your services with what corporate clients value, you stop feeling like you have to convince people. You start becoming the person they want to work with, the person they trust to make a difference.

That doesn't happen overnight – it takes focus, strategy and a willingness to step into a different way of operating – but the rewards in freedom, fulfilment and financial stability are real. It puts you in a position to build something that lasts: a business that's both proactive and sustainable, one that reflects your values, leverages your expertise and supports the kind of life you want to live.

Here's the catch. Not everyone makes this shift successfully, so let's explore why some coaches, consultants and trainers thrive in the corporate space while others, who are just as talented, keep spinning their wheels. Let's look at what makes the difference.

Why some succeed and others struggle

Many coaches, consultants and trainers land a corporate client or two but don't know how to repeat the process. The first contract is often through a personal connection or seen as being a result of luck intervening. This makes it difficult to turn the process into something predictable and repeatable.

The difference between those who build thriving businesses with corporate clients and those who don't isn't luck. It's down to positioning, being specific about who you help, the problem you solve and the resulting outcome, as well as having the right system to engage corporate decision makers in meaningful conversations. In this section, we'll look at common pitfalls that are possibly keeping you stuck and the pivotal shifts that allow some to consistently win corporate clients while others struggle.

If you've ever delivered a workshop for a corporate client but didn't get a follow-up contract, or coached a senior leader and hoped they would introduce you to their HR team, but it didn't happen, or had a corporate engagement but struggled to get another one for months, you are not alone. Many experience this exact pattern. It's frustrating because you know that corporate clients pay well, and you love the work, but the missing piece is knowing how to create a steady pipeline of opportunities. This pattern emerges because most coaches/consultants/trainers fall into the same four traps. Let's look at what those are and how you can avoid doing the same.

1. Relying on referrals and hoping for opportunities

Many coaches and consultants land their first corporate client through a personal connection but then hit a wall. They don't have a repeatable way to generate new leads and often find themselves waiting, hoping the organisation will invite them back. Without a clear strategy or practical framework for business development, opportunities show up sporadically at best.

That was me in the early days of my business. I felt I got lucky when two conversations with people in my network turned into corporate contracts, but after that, I didn't have a plan, just a whole lot of hope. The thing is, corporate decision makers are busy. Even if they love your work, they're unlikely to reach out again unless you stay visible and continue to engage with them in a way that speaks to what they care about now.

In Part Two of this book, I'll share two proactive outreach strategies that have worked not just for me, but for the coaches, consultants and trainers I've supported over the years. They are designed to help you build meaningful, long-term relationships with the right people. The aim is to be seen as someone worth listening to, someone who brings relevant insights, asks smart questions and helps decision makers think through the challenges they're facing. That's how you move beyond being a one-off supplier and start becoming a trusted partner, someone who's invited into the conversation early, whose perspective is valued and whose work is part of shaping meaningful change.

2. Looking too small or risky to corporate decision makers

When I was starting out in business I made the mistake of thinking that if I showed that I'm personable and approachable, corporates would want to work with me. I paid little attention to the fact that corporates are risk-averse. When hiring external experts they ask themselves questions like 'Can they handle this project professionally?', 'Do they have the structure to deliver results at scale?' and 'Will they still be around after one engagement?' If your LinkedIn profile or website makes you look like a solo practitioner, corporates worry that you may not have the bandwidth to support them fully.

Early on in my journey, I met with a petrochemical company who were keen to work with me. We had great conversations, they were enthusiastic, and it felt like a perfect fit. When I submitted my proposal, though, I made a mistake that cost me the contract. The proposal outlined a programme where I would deliver sessions to two groups – fifteen managers in one group and ten leaders in another. I knew I could handle the workload, as I'd already delivered multiple leadership development programmes to a number of clients consecutively, but from their side, there was a concern about what could happen if I became ill or unavailable.

I made the mistake of not including at least one other person in my proposal, even if they were only a backup. There was no indication that I had a team or a network around me who could step in if needed. To them, it looked risky, too dependent on one person. In the end, they chose a different provider. It was a tough lesson, but one that stuck with me.

When you're working with corporate clients, it's important to come across as a business, not just an individual. That doesn't mean pretending to have a huge operation. It means showing that you have a structure with the right people and the right thinking in place to deliver reliably, especially on larger projects. If you don't have a formal team, build a network of trusted associates, people you know you could call on if needed, and include their profiles in your proposal.

Make sure to include a simple line in your terms and conditions explaining that your business retains the right to deploy appropriate resources to deliver the programme as agreed. This allows you to keep control over who delivers on the day while giving the corporate decision makers confidence that there's a solid plan in place. You might still deliver the entire project yourself as planned, but if needed, you have trusted people you can call on to support part of the delivery without any drop in quality.

These two strategies are a small addition to your approach, but can make a big difference to how decision makers see you, namely not just as an individual, but as a business they can rely on.

When you're working with corporate clients, it's not just about being great at what you do, it's about giving decision makers confidence that you can deliver reliably, even if things change. By building a network of trusted associates and showing you have the right structure in place, you shift from being seen as a solo practitioner to being seen as the CEO of your business.

3. Assuming corporate clients will come back to you automatically

Many coaches, consultants and trainers assume that once they deliver a great experience, the client will keep working with them, refer them to other departments and think of them for future projects. Sometimes this happens, but not in isolation of having a follow-up strategy. Corporate decision makers are busy and overwhelmed a lot of the time. Even if they love your work, they are constantly dealing with new priorities, budget changes and internal restructures. Without a clear follow-up strategy, you will be forgotten, even if they like you.

In my Corporate Success Pathway (CSP) Programme, I teach how to deliver a strategic debrief at the end of each project as a way into the next piece of work. It goes beyond the usual feedback or evaluation report to talk through observations and insights, identifying quick wins and deeper issues that are opportunities to further help the team, department or organisation. You come across as a valuable resource, not just someone looking for more work.

When working with a corporate there will probably be a couple of key people you will work closely with on delivering a programme or project. Personnel changes can happen fast in these organisations and they won't think to tell you, so you want to make sure that you expand your network inside the organisation and are not reliant on just one or two points of contact. This happened to me when the head of learning and development and the HR director of one of my corporate clients left within the space of two months. It took me a couple of years to build relationships with their replacements and continue the work with this organisation. I now make a point of being introduced to other, connected, decision makers and staying in touch with them too.

4. Ignoring the impact of digitalisation and AI

There's another shift happening in the corporate world that you need to be aware of, one that makes it even more important to revisit your approach. More and more organisations are investing in digital platforms to deliver personalised development at scale. LinkedIn Learning, Udemy Business, Coursera for Teams and bespoke internal platforms are now commonplace. They offer employees instant access to bite-sized training, just-in-time development modules and even AI-powered career paths. Some are layering in AI coaching platforms, such as Sherlock Super Coach, that simulate coaching conversations, deliver prompts or suggest reflective practices, especially for first to mid-level managers. Others are training up internal coaches to support line managers with performance and development conversations.

These aren't just buzzwords or trends. They are strategies that are becoming embedded into how many companies deliver learning across their organisation. Where does that leave you? It means that trying to offer generic workshops or surface-level development, especially for first-time managers, is becoming less relevant. If corporates can get something that's good enough from their own system, they're unlikely to bring in an external provider. To stand out, and to be hired, you need to offer one of the following two things or maybe even both combined:

- Something that operates at a higher level. Think senior leaders navigating complexity, shaping culture or leading change. These individuals aren't served by off-the-shelf content or AI bots. They need space to reflect, test ideas and develop the thinking capacity that drives performance across the organisation. That's where high-trust partnerships matter most.

- Something that strengthens team effectiveness and adaptability. Teams need to operate with greater autonomy, work cross-functionally around key projects and adapt quickly as AI automates routine tasks. These teams don't need standard team-building exercises but practical, high-impact experiences that help them align on purpose, collaborate more effectively across functions and build the self-management skills to deliver results in fast-changing environments. This is where tailored, experiential programmes create real value.

This is where your real value lies – not in replicating what can be digitised, but in creating what can't be. When decision makers invest in external support it's no longer just about content. It's about context, insight and transformation, working with someone who understands the bigger picture and can help them think, lead and act differently. That's exactly the kind of work I'll help you shape through *The Corporate Success Pathway*.

It's worth repeating that working with corporate clients is about how you stay relevant and part of the conversation over time and having a systematic process to do so, which is what *The Corporate Success Pathway* outlines for you.

In this chapter, we've looked at the benefits of working with corporate clients and four common traps that can quietly hold even talented coaches, consultants and trainers back. None of these traps come from a lack of expertise; they come from not having the right structures and strategies in place that corporate work demands. Next, we'll explore why visibility alone is not enough and how to build trust and influence with corporate decision makers so they see you as their go-to expert, their trusted partner.

2
Visibility Is Not Enough – You Need Trust And Influence

If you've been showing up by posting regularly on LinkedIn, sending direct messages or attending networking events and are still not seeing traction with corporate clients, it can feel frustrating. You're doing what you thought you were supposed to do – being visible, offering value – so why aren't they saying yes? This chapter will show you why. The truth is, visibility alone doesn't get you hired. Not in the corporate space.

Corporate decision makers are not short on options. They're not sitting around waiting for another coach, consultant or trainer to show up in their inbox or feed. They're under pressure to solve specific, high-stakes problems and usually fast. When they're looking externally, they are not looking for 'a coach'. They're looking for someone who understands their world and can help.

They need to trust that you see the bigger picture, that you'll make their life easier, not more complicated, and they don't have time to figure out if you're that person. You might be incredibly capable but if your LinkedIn headline requires them to connect the dots, they'll move on. You can't rock up as a 'mindset coach' and expect them to figure out how that links to their retention issues or team performance challenges. That's your job.

Offer insights, not information

Corporate leaders are overwhelmed with content, data and information, but what they're hungry for is clarity, and this is where the potential partnership often breaks down. Many talented coaches, consultants and trainers hold back. They think they don't have enough experience to speak up and that other people are more experienced; they worry either that they haven't worked in a corporate leadership role so why would they be taken seriously or that they don't have a big-name client list; and they are concerned they don't bring enough to the table. I've heard all of these reasons from talented coaches, consultants and trainers, and I've even voiced some of them myself. It's important, however, to know that credibility doesn't come only from titles or a long list of client logos. It comes from relevance, from insight and from being able to articulate a problem and offer a clear, grounded path forward.

You've invested heavily in your personal and professional development. Even if you haven't worked directly with corporates, chances are you've worked with the people inside them. You've helped leaders navigate difficult conversations, grow their confidence or lead through change. That counts. If you used to work in a corporate yourself, even better. You know the rhythm, the politics, the pressures. Use that. Bring it forward in your messaging, in your stories, in the way you write and speak.

Corporates are not hiring you to 'deliver coaching', 'consult' or 'run a workshop'. They are hiring you to solve a problem, and those problems almost always connect back to one of the following four business drivers:

1. Increasing profitability – Will this make us more money / reduce costs?

2. Saving time – Will this make us more productive and efficient?

3. Reducing risk – Will this help us avoid costly mistakes, safeguard reputation, or improve decision-making in uncertain environments?

4. Navigating change and transformation – Will this help us lead change more effectively, accelerate

transformation, and build greater adaptability across the organisation?

If what you do doesn't clearly link to one or more of these, the conversation stops there. Rather than relying on the corporate decision maker to join the dots and make sense of what you are offering, why not frame what you do in this way?

For example, if you help teams improve how they communicate, that's not just supporting 'team development', that's reducing delays, misunderstandings and mistakes. If you work on leadership confidence, that's not just doing mindset work, it's enabling faster decisions, better delegation and improved team morale. If you support well-being and mental health, that's not just offering support, it's reducing burnout, sick leave and costly turnover.

Your work probably already touches on one of these drivers, you just need to say it using their language.

Once you have their attention, the next step is trust. Trust in the corporate space has three parts:

1. **Credibility:** Can you actually solve this? Do you have a track record either in results or depth of understanding?

2. **Relevance:** Do you understand their world, their industry, their culture, their pressures?

3. **Risk reduction:** Can they say yes to you without it being a headache? Do you have structure? Contingency? A clear way forward?

It's about showing up as someone who's done their homework, has a point of view and makes it easy for them to trust.

Create the room, don't wait to be invited

Even when you're credible, if you're not in the right conversations, you'll be overlooked. You know as well as I do that corporate decision makers don't tend to show up in the same spaces as small business owners. They're not at the same networking events and rarely do they sift through LinkedIn posts looking for someone to hire.

Instead of trying to find the right rooms, why not create one? The big consultancy companies such as McKinsey, Boston Consulting Group, Deloitte, PricewaterhouseCoopers and Ernst & Young have been doing this for years. They create and deliver executive round tables, invite-only forums and executive briefings. These spaces are built for insight sharing, not selling, and you can use the same principle.

You don't need to host a big fancy event. You can start with a well-crafted insight report, a small peer conversation or a topic-driven presentation with relevance to their world. More on that in Part Two, but for now, know that you don't have to sit back and hope to be discovered; you can start the conversation yourself.

In summary, if you've been putting yourself out there and are still not gaining traction with corporates, you're not doing it wrong, you're just missing a few key pieces of the puzzle. Corporates don't hire the most visible person, they hire the person who gets their world, speaks their language and solves problems they care about.

In this chapter, we've looked at how you need more than visibility to win work with corporates. You need a message that connects your work to their business priorities, clarity about the outcomes you deliver, a structure that builds trust and reduces risk and a way to be part of the right conversations without waiting for permission. There's no need to be famous and you don't need a long list of corporate clients, but you do need to show up clearly and strategically. That's exactly what we're going to explore next.

3
Why Now Is The Best Time To Make This Shift

The demand for external expertise has never been higher. Gartner and many other organisations have identified the top three issues corporates are facing in 2025 as increasing challenges in leadership effectiveness and executive development, retaining and engaging top talent, and change management and organisational transformation.[6,7] These three issues have consistently topped the list for the past two decades, and they show no signs of disappearing. That's because the pace of change isn't slowing down. If anything, the complexity facing leaders and organisations is only accelerating.

In this chapter, we'll look at these issues and help you start thinking about where your expertise can make the biggest difference.

Leadership effectiveness and executive development

Many organisations struggle with leadership gaps at all levels, leading to poor decision-making, disengagement and ineffective execution of strategy. As I talk with corporate decision makers, I regularly hear of common challenges around the following:

- Lack of future-ready leadership to handle growth and complexity

- Low executive presence and weak decision-making skills in senior leaders

- Inexperienced managers struggling to transition into leadership roles

- Lack of alignment and strategic execution across leadership teams

Recent data underscores this. According to DDI's *Global Leadership Forecast 2025*, only 20% of organisations feel confident in their leadership bench strength, indicating a significant gap in succession planning and leadership readiness.[8] The same report highlights that 71% of leaders are experiencing heightened levels of stress, and 40% have considered leaving their leadership roles to improve their well-being.

Weak leadership directly affects business performance, innovation and team effectiveness. Organisations spend millions on leadership development programmes to ensure they have the right people driving the business forward.

From my own experience, I see just how critical leadership development is to a company's success. One of our holding company clients regularly acquires new businesses to expand their portfolio. A key business-critical challenge for them is ensuring that the culture of each newly acquired company is shaped to fit the strong, healthy leadership culture of the holding company itself. There's a reason they have low talent turnover and outperform their competition, and they know that leadership and culture can't be left to chance.

We started working with them several years ago, initially supporting the leadership team at the holding company. Now every time they acquire a new company, we partner with them to further develop leadership alignment and cultural integration from the ground up. They see me and my company as a trusted partner for both one-off projects and ongoing conversations about how to progress their business success over time. Working with them gives me immense satisfaction – not just because it's provided a consistent, valuable income stream, but because it's work that makes a meaningful difference in their organisation, and they are great people to work with too.

At the end of the day, leadership effectiveness isn't a 'nice to have' – it's a foundational driver of strategic execution, innovation, employee engagement and long-term growth. If you can show corporate clients how your expertise strengthens leadership at every level, you'll be offering them a crucial competitive advantage.

Retaining and engaging top talent

Keeping talented people is one of the biggest challenges facing organisations right now. Many still feel the ripple effects of the past few years of economic uncertainty, COVID-19 lockdowns and the move to hybrid ways of working, and the transformation brought in through digitalisation and AI performing many routine tasks. The impact has been in the form of burnout, disengagement and shifting expectations, showing up in ways that affect performance, morale and long-term stability.

I hear similar concerns time and again in conversations with corporate decision makers:

- A struggle to keep hold of their best people, particularly in leadership, sales and technical roles

- A widening gap between leaders and teams, where 'them and us' thinking quietly takes hold

- Difficulty building an inclusive, high-performing culture that people genuinely want to be part of

- Employees feeling overwhelmed, stretched thin, wondering whether their job role is safe, or quietly looking for something else

You and I both know these challenges aren't just HR problems. They touch every part of the business from team dynamics and leadership effectiveness to productivity and innovation. Replacing talent is not only costly, it's disruptive. It affects trust within teams, slows down momentum and often leads to short-term fixes that don't address the root cause.

According to recent studies, replacing an employee can cost anywhere from 50% to 400% of their salary, depending on the role.[9] A mid-level manager earning £60,000 could cost the business up to £240,000 to replace once you factor in recruitment, onboarding and lost productivity.

Alongside that, global engagement levels remain low. Gallup reports that just 23% of employees worldwide are engaged in their work, while 62% are disengaged and 15% are actively disengaged. That lack of connection is estimated to cost the global economy nearly US$9 trillion in lost productivity.[10]

Burnout is still quietly undermining teams at every level. A recent study found that the cost of employee burnout can range from US$4,000 to US$21,000 per person, per year. In larger organisations, those numbers add up fast and have an impact on morale, performance and retention.[11]

That's why many organisations are investing more seriously in team effectiveness and development.

They understand that keeping great people isn't about surface-level perks, it's about creating an environment where people feel supported, seen and able to do their best work. Not all companies are truly ready to do this well, however, with some still treating it as a box-ticking exercise. You'll feel it when they hesitate to invest time or budget into meaningful change, and that's a helpful signal because you want to work with organisations that are genuinely committed.

The ones who care about their people, not just their processes, are the ones who are ready to listen, learn and lead differently. When you work with clients like that, the impact you make is deep and lasting. More than improving engagement scores, it's about helping to create the kind of workplace where people want to stay and grow – and that's work worth doing.

One of our clients, a telecoms company, knew they couldn't rely on salary increases to retain their top talent. Budgets were tight, but they still wanted to show their people they were valued and provide meaningful opportunities for growth. We worked with them to design and deliver a suite of structured leadership development programmes for different levels of management, mid-level upward, underpinned by recognised qualifications. It sent a strong signal that the organisation was committed to investing in its people and their future despite the challenging financial climate at the time.

Change management and organisational transformation

Change is no longer a one-off event; it's a constant feature of business life. Whether it's a restructure, a digital transformation, a merger or acquisition or a shift in strategic direction, most organisations are navigating some form of change at any given time, and many still struggle to get it right.

Despite decades of research and toolkits, the success rate for major change initiatives remains consistently low. Studies from organisations like McKinsey suggest that up to 70% of transformations fail to deliver their intended outcomes.[12] When they do fail, it's usually not because the strategy was wrong, but because the human side of change didn't get the attention it needed.

Here are the reasons for failure that I often hear from corporate leaders:

- Operational staff resisting change, leading to delays and disruptions

- Leaders unable to align teams behind a shared direction

- Middle managers unclear on how to support the change or communicate effectively

- Cultural mismatches that make it harder to move forward confidently

Unmanaged or poorly managed change takes a heavy toll on people, on performance and on trust, and this is where our work as coaches, consultants and trainers becomes vital.

Another of our clients, a large oil and gas company, experienced a particularly complex change. Some teams stayed, others changed entirely, and the whole organisation had to keep functioning safely and effectively throughout. There was a great deal of uncertainty. Operational staff remained in place with little change, but the supporting functions and infrastructure started shifting overnight. The company couldn't afford to lose focus, with safety and continuity as non-negotiables.

They already had one of the big consultancy firms managing the complex change process, but in my conversation with HR, we uncovered a gap, something the large firm hadn't addressed. My role wasn't to replicate their work, but to bring clarity and support in the day-to-day human experience of change. We helped the organisation take a clear pulse on morale, spotlighting where people were struggling, surfacing practical issues that could be quickly addressed and identifying areas where deeper support was needed. Alongside that, we provided structured, steady support for both staff and managers as they navigated the uncertainty.

You don't need to be a global consultancy to make a big impact. Sometimes it's precisely because you're not that you can move more quickly, be more flexible and build trust faster. Corporates don't always need bigger. They frequently need better targeted, and that's where your value lies. This is the kind of work that makes a lasting impact not just for the organisation, but for the people living through the change.

You don't need to be a corporate insider to contribute, you just need to understand what matters to these organisations and how to connect what you do to the issues they care about most. If you can speak their language, align your work to their priorities and show that you're someone who brings both clarity and calm, you'll be seen not as a service provider, but as a trusted partner. There's never been a better time to take that step.

All of your past experience – yes, even the bits that didn't quite work out – can help you build something powerful and credible in the corporate space. Why? Because nothing is ever wasted. Let's explore what you're already bringing with you.

Nothing is ever wasted

When you're thinking about stepping into the corporate space, it's easy to second-guess your background, wondering if your experience is relevant enough. If your career has zigzagged, or if you've worked mostly in the public sector or with private clients, it's easy to worry that you'll be seen as underqualified or out of place. Here's the truth: nothing you've done is ever wasted. The skills you've developed, the challenges you've worked through, the people you've supported – those all come with you. More often than not, they give you a unique edge.

I say this with confidence because I've lived it. I began my career in hospitality, with a degree in hotel and catering management. Later, I retrained in psychology and spent fourteen years working in the UK's NHS in a range of roles – managing teams and, later on, leading large transformation programmes with others. When I left the NHS, I started working with small businesses and individuals, helping them lead change and improve team performance.

At the time, I wanted to work with larger organisations, knowing they would bring a satisfaction that comes from making a bigger impact as well as improving my bottom line. I worried that my public sector background wouldn't translate, wondering if commercial corporate decision makers would take me seriously, but here's what happened. As soon as I started talking to commercial corporate leaders, I recognised the conversations. The concerns were familiar. The language was different, yes, but the underlying challenges were strikingly similar to those I'd been working on for years in the public sector and with private clients.

I went on a steep learning curve, of course, but I didn't need to start from scratch. Everything I'd done up to that point helped me relate to, understand and connect more deeply with others. Now I work comfortably across public sector, not-for-profit and commercial organisations, loving the variety and the impact it brings.

Your story will be different from mine, but the principle holds. Whether you've worked in education, creative industries, frontline services or tech start-ups, or been a leader in a large business, you've built up insight, skills and strengths that are highly relevant to corporate clients. The key is being able to see that for yourself and then helping corporate decision makers to see it too.

What I'm saying here is that your background doesn't need to be perfectly polished or traditionally 'corporate'. What matters is that you can connect what you know to the problems organisations are trying to solve. The experiences that feel unrelated often give you a valuable external perspective. They make you more human and more insightful than someone who's only ever worked within one type of organisation.

If you've ever questioned whether there's space for your work in the corporate world, I hope this chapter has helped you see that there is not just space, but a need. Organisations are under pressure. They're trying to lead more effectively in uncertain environments, they're struggling to hold on to their best people and keep them engaged, and they're navigating constant change, often without enough support for the human side of the process. These aren't abstract business challenges, they're deeply human ones, and that's where your skills, your insight and your experience come in.

You're bringing far more with you than you think. Maybe now is the time to reflect on and capture all of those far-reaching experiences you have had of leading projects and managing people. I recommend you take some time to do that now before moving on to the next chapter, where we'll address the elephant in the room: what about market downturns and economic uncertainty?

4

Navigating Uncertain Times

W hen you run your own business, economic uncertainty isn't a question of if, it's a question of when. Markets shift, industries change, and global events happen that no one can predict. In this chapter, we'll look at how to build more stability into your business, even when the market feels unpredictable. You'll see why corporate clients can provide a steadier foundation and how to position yourself to stay relevant and in demand through changing times.

I've been a business owner through more than a few times of uncertainty, and maybe you have too: the financial crisis of 2008 and 2009; the oil price crash, when prices tumbled from US$120 a barrel to just US$40, right when we had a lot of oil and gas clients in the Middle East; the COVID-19 lockdowns that swept across the world, upending everything almost overnight.

Each time, I could have looked at the headlines and thought, *That's it. Game over*, but what I've learned is that not every organisation experiences these events as disasters. Not every budget dries up and not every opportunity disappears. Some companies pull back, others adapt, invest and look for new ways forward. The key is not to assume the sky is falling, because it isn't. At least, not everywhere.

Surviving, and even thriving, through uncertain times hasn't been about chasing every possible client or dramatically changing direction (I'll spare you the word 'pivot', though you probably remember the number of times it was thrown around in 2021). It's been about staying close to what clients need in that moment. Sometimes it means reshaping offers slightly, sometimes it means being even clearer about the outcomes we can help deliver, and sometimes it simply means being there, offering stability and partnership when everything else feels unpredictable.

One of the most important lessons for me was that different sectors and industries, and even individual companies, experience downturns differently and at different times. During the financial crisis of 2008 and 2009, many corporates took a long, hard look at coaching and training budgets – often the first thing to go when looking to make cuts. We lost some clients at that time, but there were some sectors that were relatively stable and some that actually grew. Pharmacy was a big client of ours during the crisis.

Some of our oil and gas clients paused leadership development projects when oil prices dropped, but others doubled down, recognising that strong leadership would be even more critical to weathering the storm. During the lockdowns of COVID-19, we lost three big contracts with healthcare organisations. Yes, this hit us hard, but I kept reaching out to them, offering our support for their staff (unpaid), and a couple of years later, the original work came back.

It's not about panicking every time broad headlines predict a recession, and it's not about burying your head in the sand and pretending nothing is changing either. It's about staying calm, getting closer to your clients to understand how they're seeing things and looking for the opportunities that are still there, often in places you might not have expected.

Staying steady

Here's what I've found helps businesses stay steady through times of uncertainty:

- **Stay close to your clients.** Keep the conversations going. Find out what's shifting for them – not just what's being cut, but where they still have priorities and budgets. Sometimes the opportunities aren't obvious at first glance.

- **Be flexible without losing your focus.** You don't have to throw out everything you offer and start again. Often, it's a small adjustment, a change in emphasis, a slight reshaping that makes all the difference.

- **Hold your nerve.** It's easy to get spooked when the headlines are full of doom and gloom, but pulling back too quickly can mean missing the opportunities that are still there for those willing to stay steady, visible and helpful.

- **Recognise that different times create different needs.** In tougher times, organisations still invest, but they focus more sharply on what matters most: leadership, adaptability, engagement and team effectiveness. These are needs that don't go away; if anything, they become even more important.

- **Keep your perspective wide.** If one sector tightens up, others might be growing. It's worth lifting your head up and looking around. Sometimes opportunity comes from a direction you hadn't been focusing on before.

- **Tighten up your terms and conditions**, particularly around cancellations. Make sure you have payment terms where you are paid in full, or at least a large percentage, before the first day of delivery, particularly for longer programmes that may be postponed part way through when things change.

It's easy to see downturns as all risk and no reward, and yes, some opportunities shrink, but new ones open up too. Organisations still have problems to solve. They still need to adapt, to lead, to deliver and they still need trusted partners to help them do it.

The businesses that keep moving through uncertain times aren't necessarily the biggest or the flashiest. They're the ones that stay connected to their clients, listen well, respond thoughtfully and stay visible in the right way. You don't have to predict exactly what's going to happen, but you do have to stay close enough to notice what's shifting and respond without losing who you are. In the end, economic downturns are part of the rhythm of running a business. They can feel unsettling but they don't have to stop you moving forward.

By staying connected, making thoughtful adjustments and keeping your focus on what matters most to your clients, you give yourself the best chance not just to keep going, but to grow, even when the market feels unpredictable. Remember: every period of change brings new opportunities if you stay open to them. You don't need to reinvent yourself overnight. You just need to stay steady, stay connected and move forward with clarity and care.

Now that we understand that preparation, insight and communication are key to successfully navigating uncertainty, let's summarise what we've learned.

The journey so far

Over the past few chapters, you've been invited to look at corporate work through a different lens – one that moves away from myths and assumptions to what really drives decisions inside organisations.

You've seen that winning corporate clients isn't about luck or having the right connections. It's about trust and aligning with business priorities.

You've recognised that corporates don't just want services, they want solutions to the problems that matter most to them: solutions that improve performance, reduce costs, move through a major change and help them reduce risk. You've understood that it's not about shouting the loudest but about being relevant, offering insight and creating conversations that lead somewhere meaningful.

If you've ever questioned whether you have the right background or track record, you've realised that what matters most is being the right fit for the challenge at hand. This is a shift in perspective and one that unlocks possibility, because when you stop chasing visibility and start focusing on engaging the right people in meaningful ways, things start to shift in your business.

In Part Two, you'll learn how to turn these realisations into a consistent, repeatable approach to corporate work. You'll no longer be just hoping corporate clients will come your way. You will be ready to take the lead with a clear pathway in front of you.

PART TWO
THE CORPORATE SUCCESS PATHWAY METHOD

One of the most common things I hear from coaches, consultants and trainers when they first come to work with me is: 'I know I want corporate clients, but I just don't know how to get them.'

When people talk about working with corporates, it can sound vague, like something you're supposed to just 'figure out' as you go. One day you're questioning your pricing, the next you're wondering if your offer is right, and then you're not sure who you should even be speaking to. It can all feel a bit scattered. Getting corporate clients doesn't need to feel as hit-and-miss as this. In this part of the book, I'll introduce a clear, step-by-step pathway to help you consistently win corporate work, without second-guessing yourself every time you reach out to a corporate decision maker.

Winning corporate clients isn't about being lucky, although I get why it can feel that way. It's not about knowing the 'right people', having the fanciest credentials or sending out 100 cold emails and hoping one lands. It is about having a clear, repeatable system, one that positions you as a valuable partner (not just a service provider), makes your services an easy yes for decision makers and fills your pipeline with opportunities that actually lead somewhere.

Maybe you have dipped a toe in already, and worked with a corporate client or two, delivered a one-off session or short engagement... and then it stopped there. You can't quite explain how those clients came about (usually a personal connection or a bit of word-of-mouth magic), and it often feels impossible to repeat. Maybe you have reached out to corporates and been met with silence or had hopeful conversations with lovely, enthusiastic middle managers who say all the right things... and then can't get anything signed off beyond a short workshop or a coaching assignment. Sound familiar?

It's not that your work isn't good enough or that you're not credible, capable or experienced. It's just that you've never been shown how this world works or how to enter it with a clear plan. This changes when you see and understand the CSP.

5
A Five-Step Model For Success

In this chapter, we'll take an overall look at the Corporate Success Pathway – a five-step model that moves you from sporadic corporate projects to a steady pipeline of high-value corporate clients. It eliminates the guesswork and gives you a clear structure to follow. These five steps work together to create a repeatable approach that helps you attract, secure and grow your business with corporate clients by focusing on the things that actually matter: being seen as credible, offering structured services, pricing with confidence, connecting with the right decision makers and building trusted relationships. They create a clear, repeatable rhythm that brings you corporate opportunities in a way that's grounded, strategic and authentic to you.

The five steps are:

1. Position – how you are perceived by corporate decision makers

2. Package – how your services are structured and outcome-focused

3. Price – how your fees align with the value you deliver

4. Prospect – how you identify the right organisations and decision makers

5. Promote – how you build trust and open doors to meaningful conversations

Now, you might be looking at those five steps and thinking that it sounds a bit like every marketing course you've ever done. At first glance, I get that: the words themselves aren't new. How we use them here, however, is. What makes the CSP different is that it's built specifically for coaches, consultants and trainers who want to work primarily with corporate clients, not private clients or small businesses. This isn't about funnels or clever marketing tricks – it's about strategy that works in the corporate world. It's about understanding how corporates think, what they value and how to meet them at the level of strategic partnership, not with a sales pitch. Most decision makers actively dislike being sold to. They don't want to be pitched at or persuaded; they want to engage with people who understand their world, bring useful insights to the table, and offer practical solutions to real business challenges.

Here's how these steps shift when you apply them in the corporate space:

- Position isn't about catchy headlines. It's about being seen as someone who gets their organisational world and solves real problems.

- Package isn't about productising your services. It's about creating outcome-based offers that make it easy for organisations to say yes, and say yes again.

- Price isn't about charging what you're worth. It's about aligning your fees with business outcomes and presenting them in a way that makes sense to corporate buyers.

- Prospect isn't about casting a wide net. It's about identifying the right people in the right organisations who have the authority and urgency to act.

- Promote isn't about shouting louder. It's about creating conversations that build trust and lead to meaningful opportunities.

Yes, you may have heard some of these words before, but in this book you'll work with them through a fresh lens. You don't have to figure this out alone. In the chapters ahead, we'll walk through each step of the pathway with a blend of structure and room to make it your own. We'll break down the steps in detail with practical strategies, real-world examples and insights you can apply right away. You'll find examples, reflection prompts and encouragement along the way. This is about helping you shift from wondering where your next corporate client might come from to feeling clear, confident and in control of your business development.

The Corporate Success Pathway is not a magic bullet

Let's be honest about the process. The CSP isn't a shortcut. It's a structured, repeatable system that brings consistency and clarity, but it still takes time.

On average, it takes about ninety days from first connection to delivering a piece of work with corporates. Most of the people you speak to won't be ready to buy straight away. Most will be in the 'ready-soon' or 'ready-later' category, or even 'ready-when' something happens. That's how it works, and internal conversations take time with multiple people involved. This isn't a problem, it's part of how corporate decisions are made, which is why you need more than a handful of conversations on the go. You need a system that keeps you visible, credible and connected. The CSP helps you build a rhythm that puts you in front of the right people again and again, in a way that's sustainable.

There's no need to become proficient in every step of the pathway before getting started. In fact, holding back until everything feels 'finished' often just delays the learning that comes from real-world engagement. The most resonant positioning and the most effective packages often emerge through conversations that help you hear what matters most and adjust your approach accordingly.

Even after twenty years of working with corporate clients, I still refine and reshape our positioning and packages. Needs evolve and language shifts. The work is always in motion, and that's exactly as it should be. Some words and phrases become overused to the point of being almost meaningless or irritating. You want to adapt and refine as you go along. Keep moving because you'll find clarity through doing, not through waiting, and you already have enough to begin.

While progress might feel slow or uncertain at times, it's important to remember why you're doing this in the first place. Let's explore what makes it all worth it – the broader view of building a business with corporate clients.

The bigger picture

Let's take a moment to step back from the process and look at where it leads. You probably, like me, set off down this path of business ownership with a desire for more freedom, not just in how you spend your time, but in how you shape your future. You wanted the autonomy to make your own decisions, to choose who you work with and to no longer have someone else dictate how your talents get used. That freedom isn't just about working fewer hours or being your own boss. It's about building a business that feels meaningful, sustainable and genuinely yours.

Having consistent corporate clients can help make that possible – not through one-off wins, but by giving your business the revenue, structure and confidence to grow in a way that supports the life you want.

Here's what the benefits look like in real terms.

1. Higher fees and longer engagements

Working with corporates changes the economics of your business. Coaching a couple of leaders in an organisation can bring in anywhere from £6,000 to £12,000. A six- to nine-month leadership development programme for one group of leaders can range from £50,000 to £100,000. I hope you can see that you don't need dozens of clients to achieve your revenue goals. Just a few of these engagements can take your business well into six figures with far more breathing space than chasing one-off projects or working with private individuals or small businesses ever will.

2. Predictability

Corporate clients often bring you back again and again, especially when you build in strategic debriefs and offer natural follow-on work after a successful programme or consulting engagement. You're not constantly starting from scratch – you're creating a rhythm, a steady stream of work and relationships that deepen over time. For example, my company has partnered with a large healthcare organisation with over 15,000 employees for the past fourteen years. What began as a handful of their staff attending a three-day leadership programme has evolved into hundreds progressing through various levels of our ILM qualifications in leadership and management.

What the organisation values about our partnership is our deep understanding of their organisational context and the challenges they face. They were seeking a development partner who could align with their strategic goals and adapt to their evolving needs. By consistently delivering relevant and impactful programmes, we've built a relationship based on trust and mutual growth. More than being about repeat business, this kind of long-term engagement is about becoming a trusted partner who evolves alongside the client, providing solutions that are both timely and tailored.

3. Bigger impact

You already understand the ripple effect of your work; whether it's coaching a private client or supporting a small business, you've seen how insights and shifts cascade outward. When you work with larger organisations, that ripple becomes a wave. As well as supporting individuals, you are strengthening teams, shaping systems and influencing how the organisation functions day-to-day. When you help leaders to communicate more effectively, teams to collaborate more smoothly or processes to align more closely with strategic goals, those shifts reach across departments, and they last.

Your impact is amplified not because you are doing more, but because the changes you help bring about ripple through systems and structures as well as individuals. More than solving a problem, you are helping shape how the organisation leads, performs and evolves over time. That is the beginning of legacy.

4. Leveraging relationships

One of the most powerful, and often underestimated, aspects of corporate work is what happens when people move. When you've built trusted relationships and delivered meaningful results, clients often take you with them. A lovely example of this is a woman I'll call Rachel (not her real name). She first joined one of our leadership development programmes at the company she was working for at the time. Thoughtful and committed, she later took part in a coaching programme we also ran in the same company, which was a turning point that helped her step into a more senior role with greater confidence and clarity.

When Rachel moved to a new organisation and a more senior role, she didn't just remember the content, she remembered how she had felt seen, supported and stretched. When the CEO and COO of her new organisation were looking for someone to work with their leadership team, a team navigating major change and in real need of cohesion, she introduced me. They were looking for a safe pair of hands, not just another provider – someone who could build trust quickly and bring the team together in a meaningful way.

That one introduction led to multiple engagements across several companies and continues to this day.

This kind of continuity doesn't come from transactional delivery. It grows from connection, trust and the care you bring to every piece of work. The relationships you build today often become the bridges to tomorrow's opportunities, sometimes years down the line, but you need to know how to nurture these relationships.

5. More freedom and flexibility

As your work with corporate clients grows, so does your capacity to shape how your business runs. You begin to see the potential for a steadier flow of work, built on relationships, trust and meaningful conversations. This opens up new possibilities. For some, it may mean bringing in associates or collaborators to help deliver larger projects so you can focus on higher-value work or simply reduce your delivery load. For others, it might mean refining things so you can work fewer days, with fewer clients, and still earn well.

Not everyone wants to scale, and not everyone should. What most people want is choice: the ability to say yes or no, to shape their week intentionally and to step off the treadmill of constantly having to re-start the pipeline. This is about building a business that truly works for you, one that gives you space to grow in the way you want to grow, one where you're well paid for your expertise, trusted by clients and free to do your best work without burning out. The CSP helps make that possible.

The Corporate Success Scorecard

Before we dive into each of the five steps of the CSP, let's pause for a quick check-in. By now, you've seen the bigger picture. You know what's possible when you build a business that consistently serves corporate clients in terms of revenue and reach, and also in terms of freedom, fulfilment and creating something on your own terms. The next step is to figure out where you are right now, so you can focus your time and energy in the most useful places. That's what the Corporate Success Scorecard is for. It is a simple but powerful tool I've devised to support you on the CSP to help you get a clear view of where you are right now across the five steps. It will help you assess your current strengths, spot any gaps and get clarity on which steps will move you closer to landing consistent, rewarding corporate work.

The scorecard isn't a pass/fail exercise, and it's not about getting the 'right' answer. It's about helping you notice where you are strong and grounded, where you are unsure or underdeveloped and where to begin, or where to revisit, as you move through this book.

You may find that you're clear on how to position your expertise, but not yet confident in your pricing. Maybe you've got great packages, but you're not quite sure how to identify the right people to speak to. This gives you a way to focus so you're not just reading through the chapters, but actively using them to move your business forward.

Take the Corporate Success Scorecard online. It takes less than five minutes and gives you a simple break-down of your current strengths and areas for development across the five steps of the CSP, providing a useful baseline to come back to as you move through the rest of the book and start putting things into action. You'll get a simple score for each area and an individualised report with a few gentle pointers on what to focus on next.

Once you've taken the quiz, use your results to guide how you move through Part Two. You're welcome to go through each chapter in order (they're designed to flow well that way), but if your score shows that a particular step needs attention, it's perfectly fine to jump straight there.

Just be honest with yourself. This is your business, your rhythm, your next chapter.

Take the scorecard here:

https://corporatesuccess.scoreapp.com

Congratulations on Completing the Scorecard!

Your full report has been emailed to noone@zmail.com. Change email address

You've taken an important step towards securing more corporate clients. Dive into your personalised feedback below to discover actionable insights and strategies tailored to your unique strengths and opportunities.

● low   ● medium   ● high

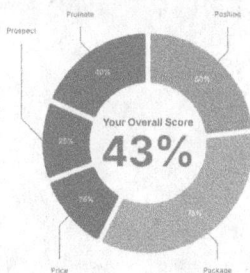

Your Overall Score

43%

Now take a moment to consider your scorecard results by answering the following questions:

- Which area of the CSP feels most developed for you right now?

- Which area feels like it needs more clarity or attention?

- What would feel like meaningful progress over the next thirty days?

There's no rush. Use this as a guide and remember that you don't have to address everything at once – you just need to keep moving forward. In this chapter, you've learned what the five steps are. Now you're ready to look in more detail at each of them, and we'll begin with Step 1, the foundation for everything else to come.

6
Step 1: Position

If you want to win corporate work consistently and not just occasionally, how you're positioned in the minds of decision makers is everything. It's about how clearly and confidently you show up in the market and how quickly a corporate buyer can see that you solve a specific business problem they care about. In this chapter, we'll unpick how you do that.

Many coaches, consultants and trainers I work with are not early in their journey. They've often delivered excellent work, even within a couple of corporates, but either the work hasn't led to repeat business or they're not gaining traction with new clients. They might be visible, even respected in their circles, but something isn't translating into consistent opportunities. More often than not, it's a positioning issue.

Let's start by clearing something up.

- Positioning is how you're perceived by the market – your strategic place in the mind of your ideal client.

- Messaging is how you communicate that positioning – through your words, content and conversations.

Without strong positioning, even the sharpest messaging will fall flat. Corporate decision makers don't base their buying decisions on how well you explain your process or how many certifications you hold. They base it on perceived relevance, confidence that you can deliver the results and clarity on your structure of delivery. They are looking for someone who understands their world and their problems, and can credibly help them move forward.

Positioning isn't just strategic, it's also personal. If you're building a business for the long haul, your positioning needs to reflect both what the market wants and what lights you up. When I first started out, I offered a wide mix of services, trying to see what would work. I coached, consulted on change and transformation and trained on topics like problem-solving, decision-making and communication skills. Like many of us, I said yes to a lot. I was good at those things, and they got results, but over time I noticed something important. The work that truly energised and inspired me was developing leaders and working with leadership teams to navigate change.

Delivering training on problem-solving and decision-making didn't light me up. Supporting a leadership team through transformation? That's where I came alive, so I paid attention. I refined my positioning to focus clearly and confidently on leadership development, and it stuck. My company has been known for that ever since.

Positioning isn't just about narrowing your expertise. It's about aligning your business with the work you're best at and want more of. That's what helps you build a reputation that lasts.

Key components of positioning for corporates

Corporate decision makers are busy; they don't have time to decode vague messaging or guess at what you do. If they don't quickly see who you help, what problem you solve and what outcome you deliver, they move on. This is why we focus this chapter on the WPO model, which comprises these three steps:

1. **Who** you help. Who do you work with? Not 'organisations' or 'teams', but which roles, in what industries, at what stage of growth? In other words, this is about specificity. Don't

worry if this feels a big leap; we'll step through this starting with thinking about industries and sectors that are relevant for you, the types of organisations best suited to your experience, and the job roles or departments that make sense.

2. The **problem** you solve. What problem are they already grappling with? Is it underperforming teams? Talent retention? Burnout in middle management? Sluggish sales pipelines? Make it unmistakable and this gives an urgent sense of relevance.

3. The **outcome** you deliver. What happens when you've done your job well? What changes? What becomes possible? Craft an outcome orientation that corporate decision makers understand. This is what sits at the heart of the WPO model and helps you become memorable, trusted and credible.

Which industries are best for you?

With so many choices, it can feel overwhelming, so let's bring this back to you.

Your background and experience

Often coaches, consultants and trainers discount the world they've come from when they set themselves up in business. I get it. You left your job for a reason, but the truth is, you understand the language, the systems and, most importantly, the challenges of that industry. Why wouldn't you use that wealth of experience now?

You may worry that going back into that world feels like a step backward, but you're not going back as an employee. You're moving forward as a business owner, a peer to the corporate decision makers you work with. This is your opportunity to reclaim that expertise and use it in a way that works for you.

What industries do you know from the inside? Who are the suppliers or adjacent sectors where your understanding of challenges and language still applies?

Your wider interests and values

You don't have to be limited to where you've come from. Sometimes there's a strong pull towards a particular type of organisation because of a shared experience, value set or interest. Take Mary (not her real name), a client of mine. She's a coach and trainer specialising in leadership development. There is a charity that held a special place in her heart, but she hesitated. She wasn't sure they'd take her seriously. She worried she wasn't corporate enough, and she didn't know how to structure an offer that would resonate with them. Beneath her hesitation was a deeper doubt: *Who am I to approach an organisation I care so much about?*

77

What Mary brought, and what made the difference, was a depth of connection to the work and the people. Her strength wasn't in having polished, perfect positioning. It was in being clear, honest and genuinely aligned. She didn't need to overthink or over-professionalise – she just needed to lead with clarity and care.

With a little encouragement, she reached out to the CEO. That first conversation was nerve-racking but authentic, and that authenticity landed. This led to a series of projects where she supported the charity in empowering leaders throughout the organisation. It didn't happen all at once. What began with hesitation grew into a deeply fulfilling partnership because she followed what mattered to her and trusted that her connection to the mission was enough.

Mary has delved more deeply into the importance of working with values-led organisations and this is now reflected more fully in her positioning. What could it be for you?

Why positioning isn't just logical

Corporate buyers appear rational, but even for them buying decisions are always emotional first. They're asking:

- Do I trust this person?

- Do they understand our reality?

- Will this make me look like I've made a smart choice, minimised risk and delivered something that gets noticed?

That third question is particularly important. The reputation of the person bringing you into the organisation is on the line far more than yours is. This is a key difference between working with private individuals or small business owners and working with corporate decision makers. If they get it wrong, it reflects directly on their judgement, so the stakes are higher.

With this in mind, it's only after those emotional boxes are ticked that they look at your case studies, credentials or frameworks. Your positioning needs to give them that emotional green light that you're someone who gets it, before their brain kicks in to justify the choice.

A REAL EXAMPLE: Positioning

Sue (not her real name) was a capable, qualified leadership coach but she was feeling stuck. She had worked with a few clients in the corporate space, but it wasn't translating into ongoing work or new opportunities. She couldn't understand why. She kept thinking, *I know I'm good at what I do, so why aren't decision makers seeing it?*

Her original positioning was centred around helping female leaders become more confident. This was a meaningful intention, but it wasn't resonating with the corporate clients she wanted to reach. She was pouring energy into content, having well-intentioned conversations and getting polite interest – but without any follow-up. Beneath it all was a growing sense of frustration and doubt.

Through our work together, we uncovered something important. Sue had deep insight into the financial services sector. She understood the pace, the politics and the pressures, especially for senior women trying to lead with influence in male-dominated environments. That was the real edge.

We refined her positioning to reflect that: 'My clients call on me when senior women are battling imposter syndrome and struggling to lead with authority after stepping into higher-stakes roles. They want to see these leaders thrive with confidence, influence and impact.'

That clarity gave her confidence. It shaped how she talked about her work, the examples she shared and the packages she created. Within months, she'd landed contracts with two major financial institutions, not because she changed who she was, but because her positioning finally reflected the depth and relevance of what she brought to the table.

Pitfalls to avoid

If you've been in business for a while, you may fall back on doing what's worked before, but this often doesn't work in a corporate context. Even smart, experienced coaches, consultants and trainers get caught in these five common traps:

1. Mistaking visibility for positioning. You're showing up on LinkedIn, you're creating content, but if your message isn't anchored in a clear position, you're building noise, not traction.

2. Describing your process instead of the business problem. You talk about coaching models, assessment tools or frameworks but not the organisational pain points they solve. Corporate decision makers care about outcomes first over your method.

3. Trying to sound clever instead of being clear. Long words, jargon and complex concepts can feel impressive, but they create friction. Decision makers don't have time to interpret what you've written or said. If they don't get what you do in seconds, they'll move on.

4. Assuming your experience speaks for itself. You've got credentials, years in the industry and glowing feedback. That matters but only after a buyer understands what you do and why it's relevant. You still need clear, confident positioning.

5. Being too broad or 'for everyone'. If you try to appeal to everyone with the messages 'I help businesses grow' and 'I work with leaders at all levels', you end up resonating with no one. Corporate clients trust specialists, not generalists.

Your turn: Applying these principles to your business

Now that you've seen how powerful positioning can be and the pitfalls to avoid, let's apply these principles to your own business. Clarity, specificity and differentiation are what make corporate decision makers take notice. To help you craft or refine a suitable positioning statement, let's work through a few key questions. Grab a pen and a notebook, or use your phone or whatever your preferred method of note-taking is, and write down your thoughts. Let's start shaping a positioning statement that truly sets you apart.

Use the prompts below to develop your positioning statement.

Establish what type of work lights you up

Answer the questions below and use these insights to guide your positioning. This isn't about narrowing who you are, it's about owning what you love.

- Which parts of your work energise you – even when they stretch you?

- What kinds of problems do you love helping organisations solve?

- What do you want to be doing more of, five years from now?

Build your positioning statement using the WPO model

Who do you help?

- What industry or sector do you serve or want to serve? Think about your past experiences in industries you know and understand as well as your interests.

- What type of organisations do you work with or want to work with? What's their focus or sector? Which sectors make sense given your experience? For example, you may have come from, or enjoy, working with dynamic and high-pressured environments. There's a broad range of sectors that experience these types of environments, eg healthcare, finance and technology. What fits with your experience and interests?

- What job roles or departments do you typically work with or want to work with? Think about the sorts of problems that you love solving and where they might show up most in an organisation. Is it with mid-level managers, senior leaders or maybe it's department specific like sales teams.

Now write your answer in the format of 'I help [specific audience] in [industry/sector].'

What **problem** do they face?

- What challenges do your clients struggle with before they work with you?

- What is the pain point or trigger moment that makes them seek help?

Now write your answer in the format of 'They come to me when they struggle with [specific problem or challenges].'

What **outcomes** do you deliver?

- What results do your clients achieve after working with you?

- How does their business, teams or performance improve?

Now write your answer in the format of 'I help them achieve [specific outcome].'

Finalise your positioning statement

Now combine your answers into one clear positioning statement: 'I help [specific audience] in [industry/sector] who come to me when they struggle with [specific problem/challenge] to achieve [specific outcome].'

You could also try this: 'My clients call on me when they [problem or challenge] and they want to achieve [outcome].'

Here are a few examples:

'I help B2B sales teams in telecoms shorten sales cycles and close more enterprise deals by becoming expert in a consultative selling approach.'

'I help operational leaders in logistics companies streamline underperforming processes and embed continuous improvement practices that reduce cost and boost team efficiency.'

'I equip mid-level managers in the healthcare sector with the communication and leadership skills needed to navigate high-pressure environments and build cohesive, high-performing teams.'

Say your version out loud. How does that feel? Test it out on people in your network and get feedback.

This is not a one-and-done task but one to come back to and refine as you engage with corporate decision makers and learn the nuances of their language, how they talk about their challenges and the outcomes that truly matter to them. Remember: this can also change over time.

Final thoughts: Why positioning changes everything

This step is about owning the space you want to occupy clearly, consistently and confidently. When your positioning is strong and your messaging is in alignment, you get into better conversations, faster, and you stop trying to prove yourself. After all, you want to be seen for what you already do brilliantly.

Now that we've clarified your position in the market, it's time to shape your expertise into structured service packages that are easy for corporate clients to say yes to. In Step 2, we'll look at how to make your work not only desirable but buyable.

7
Step 2: Package

N ow that you have established your positioning in Step 1, the next step is turning your expertise into structured, outcome-driven service packages that corporates will buy. In other words, create corporate-friendly offers with clear deliverables and outcomes. This chapter will help you define and structure packages that are easy to understand, flexible to deliver, commercially viable and aligned with organisational needs.

Remember: corporate decision makers are risk-averse and outcome-driven. They don't invest in vague coaching, training or consulting services. They are looking for clear, structured solutions that address specific business challenges. They expect you to lead the process and define the structure, but they also need to feel involved in co-creating the solution to ensure their buy-in. It's a delicate balance between standardisation and customisation: providing enough structure to instil confidence in your expertise while allowing enough flexibility for them to contribute to, refine and take ownership of the outcome. When they feel invested, they're more likely to champion your solution and sell the idea to others involved in the decision-making process of hiring you.

Two tiers: Quick win versus signature programme

One of the most effective ways to package your services for corporates is to offer two levels of engagement:

1. A smaller, quick-win option that delivers value fast and reduces perceived risk.

2. A longer, deeper option that addresses root causes and creates meaningful, strategic change. This will probably be your signature programme.

Quick win

This is typically where new corporate clients begin. It gives them a chance to experience how you work and see results quickly. This is smaller in scope but still designed to solve a problem; for example, coaching a couple of leaders to address a specific leadership challenge; a two-day workshop, or equivalent split over a few weeks, on a priority topic (for example, leading through change, having difficult conversations); a needs assessment for a team or function, followed by a short report with observations and practical recommendations.

These packages work best when they're tightly scoped and easy to implement. They reduce perceived risk for the client while giving you insight into the organisation and can often pave the way for deeper work by building a strategic debrief at the end of every engagement.

Signature programme

This is your core offer, the one you want to become known for. It goes deeper into the root issues, builds capability over time and aligns with strategic priorities. Examples of signature programmes could be a six-month leadership development programme with taught modules, one-to-one coaching and internal project work; a detailed organisational needs assessment followed by delivery of the implementation plan addressing gaps in specific systems and processes; a blended learning journey combining workshops, coaching, diagnostics and peer learning to support a major change initiative and improve team effectiveness.

These programmes solve bigger problems, generate wider impact and give you the opportunity to embed change. They are also easier to resell internally and expand across the business once proven.

When speaking with decision makers and co-creating a solution, I'll often ask if they are looking for a quick win or a deeper solution to an underlying issue. It helps clarify what they need right now, without pressure, and it also positions me as someone with range and structure, not someone showing up to 'see what sticks'.

A note on advanced options

Once a client has worked with you and seen the value you bring, they'll often ask 'What else can you help us with?' That's your invitation to explore a more advanced, strategic offer – whether that's scaling a programme across departments, offering executive advisory support or designing a bespoke initiative based on broader needs.

Remember: you don't need to build this third tier straight away. Start with two well-structured offers that solve problems and allow your advanced offer to emerge through experience and client trust.

We explore how to develop this advanced tier in more depth, including how to run a strategic debrief and a capabilities briefing that open up wider conversations with the organisation, in our CSP Programme. If this is something you'd like to find out more about, details are provided at the end of this book.

Surviving in a world of AI and online platforms

As I mentioned in an earlier chapter of the book, corporates are increasingly turning to scalable solutions to develop their people – for example, LinkedIn Learning, internal training portals and AI coaching. These platforms are cost-effective, always-on and good enough for many routine needs. What that means for you is that your packages need to stand apart not just in content but in strategic value. To be compelling in today's market, your packages must do one of these two things and, ideally, both:

1. Reach higher. Offer something for leaders and decision makers navigating complexity, change and growth. These are people AI cannot coach effectively; they need human insight, challenge and partnership.

2. Go deeper. Offer something that is experimental, contextual and tailored. Something that solves real problems in real time. Think stakeholder alignment, team effectiveness, cultural nuance or leading through transformation.

You are not here to replicate what they already have access to. You are here to deliver what they can't get anywhere else.

Key components of an attractive service package

Corporate decision makers don't buy coaching, consulting or training; they buy confidence, clarity and a sense that they're making the right investment. That means your offer needs to do more than simply describe what you do. It needs to clearly outline what you deliver, how it's structured and what success will look like on the other side. Let's walk through the components that make a package not only attractive but easy to buy. You can apply this process to both quick-win options and your signature programme.

1. A clear and compelling name

Here, we are looking for a name that communicates the value and outcome corporates will experience from the delivery of your solution. Strong names help the decision maker imagine the results. For example:

- The Executive Fast-Track Programme – a coaching programme for newly promoted executives

- The High-Impact Leadership Accelerator – a structured leadership development programme for mid-level managers

- Strategic HR Advisory – consulting for HR leaders on talent retention and succession planning

Using action-oriented words such as 'accelerator', 'fast-track' or 'transformation' helps make your packages stand out and speaks to corporate decision makers' need for speed.

2. A defined audience

A strong corporate package clearly states who it is for, helping decision makers quickly determine if it is relevant to their organisation. Here are some examples:

- For mid-level managers: 'A coaching and training programme to help mid-level managers transition into leadership roles with confidence.'

- For sales directors: 'A sales transformation programme for outbound sales teams to shorten sales cycles and improve close rates.'

- For HR leaders: 'A strategic advisory for HR leaders to retain talent and strengthen succession planning.'

Avoid saying 'for everyone'. Some skill sets, such as conflict resolution, are generic and everyone needs them, but the more specific you are, the more valuable it appears.

3. The core problem you solve

Corporates invest in services that solve clear pressing problems, not broad aspirations. Think about what business challenge your solutions help overcome and what happens if the organisation doesn't address this issue.

Here are a few examples:

- Problem: High turnover among new managers leads to poor team performance.

  Solution: 'The High-Impact Leadership Accelerator helps new managers build confidence and leadership skills, reducing attrition and improving team engagement.'

- Problem: Sales teams are struggling to close enterprise deals.

  Solution: 'The Enterprise Sales Blueprint Programme trains sales professionals in consultative selling to increase deal conversion rates.'

- Problem: Operational inefficiencies across departments are increasing costs and slowing delivery timelines.

  Solution: 'The Operational Excellence Partnership provides a structured diagnostic and transformation plan to streamline processes, reduce waste and improve cross-functional performance.'

By framing the problem in business terms, not personal development, you are appealing to what corporates care about: performance, retention, profitability and risk reduction.

4. A defined transformation and business outcome

When I'm meeting with corporate decision makers and we are co-creating a solution for their business challenge, I often ask them, 'What would success look like?' They talk about tangible results they would like to see and experience after engaging me and my team. This is what they ultimately care about. Make sure, therefore, that your package outlines what success looks like using their words. Think about what success would look like for your corporate clients and how they would express this.

For example:

- 'By the end of this programme, your mid-level managers will have the skills to lead with confidence, resulting in higher talent retention and improved team productivity.'

- 'This training will reduce the average sales cycle from six months to three months by equipping your team with advanced negotiation skills.'

- 'By the end of this engagement, your operations team will have identified and resolved key bottlenecks in their workflow, leading to a 20%

improvement in project delivery time and clearer cross-department accountability.'

If you have quantifiable results, use them; for example, increase retention by 15% or boost leadership confidence scores by 30%. If you don't have quantifiable results, start collecting that data; the organisations you are working with may well be collecting useful data that you could use. For example, one of our clients, who we had delivered leadership development programmes to for the past four years at that point, happened to mention that 43% of all participants on our programmes had been promoted into more senior roles within the space of twelve months of completion. That is an incredible result for them and a great data point that I now leverage in our marketing.

5. A clear structure and delivery format

Corporate decision makers need to be able to visualise how the programme works before they invest. This includes having a clear timeline, process and deliverables. I often provide this as both a list and in a visual form as a roadmap or journey in proposals to make it more understandable.

A delivery format could be workshops and training in the form of in-person or virtual sessions over a set period. (Side note: hybrid sessions where you have some participants attending in person and some attending virtually are not effective and are distracting for both audiences, so avoid this where you can.) It could be one-to-one or group coaching in the form of weekly or monthly coaching engagements, or it could be consulting or advisory support in the form of ongoing strategic guidance with defined check-ins. You could offer a full consulting process that takes the client through the different stages of needs discovery, recommendations, implementation and evaluation.

Let's look at an example of a structured package.

Package	The High-Impact Leadership Accelerator
Duration	Six months
Format	Six interactive workshops, each of two days
	One-to-one coaching support between sessions
Delivery	Virtual or in person
Key takeaways	Increased leadership confidence, better team engagement, reduced turnover

You want to avoid selling sessions or hours and instead sell a structured process that delivers results.

6. A clear pricing model

We'll cover this in more detail in Step 3, but remember that corporate clients need clear pricing, whether as a project fee, a per-cohort cost or a retainer model. Here are some examples:

- '£30,000 for a six-month executive coaching programme for up to ten leaders.'

- '£42,000 for a three-month operational review and transformation plan across two departments, including diagnostic interviews, process mapping and strategic recommendations with an implementation roadmap.'

- '£8,500 monthly retainer for coaching up to five executives, including unlimited email support and quarterly leadership workshops.'

Remember: you are not selling time, you are selling value and transformation.

7. Proof as case studies

Corporate decision makers often need proof that your solution works before investing. If you haven't delivered your programme to a large organisation, you can still use data and feedback you have from smaller or private clients. If you are using a particular framework, model or approach, you can use their data and results as an example of 'typical results' from these types of programmes.

The structure for your case studies that works with corporates is this:

The challenge	'A global tech company was struggling with leadership retention.'	'A national logistics company was facing rising operational costs and delays due to inefficiencies across multiple departments.'
The solution	'We implemented our High-Impact Leadership Accelerator Programme with six months of training and coaching.'	'We conducted a three-month consulting engagement that included cross-functional diagnostics, process mapping and a transformation plan with phased implementation.'
The results	'Turnover among first-time managers decreased by 20% and employee engagement scores improved by 18%.'	'Operational costs were reduced by 12% within six months, and project delivery times improved by an average of 18% across the two key business units.'

Remember: concrete results equal higher trust.

Presentation of your packages

It is useful to have various forms of your packages and I would recommend working with a graphic designer or AI to produce a polished, professional presentation. This might be in the form of a one-pager – a simple

PDF outlining the package, benefits and key details; a presentation slide deck to use as a basis in your proposal documents; or a website 'Services' page – a dedicated section clearly explaining your corporate offers in broad terms (you do not need to include prices).

An important point to remember is *not* to send out your one-pager or presentation slide deck to corporate decision makers as part of your marketing. Be strategic about sharing your one-pager. Take it into meetings with you and use it as part of the conversation, as a foundation to co-create the perfect solution with that particular corporate. Then make amendments to your presentation slide deck and include the relevant slides in your proposal document.

Here's an example of an offer using all of the seven components:

Name of package	Confident Leaders, Thriving Teams
Audience	Mid-level managers in tech companies
Core problem you solve	Underperforming teams, leadership gaps, talent retention
Outcome	Improved leadership confidence, higher team engagement, reduced turnover by 20%
Format	Strengths assessment; leadership competency assessment before and after programme; three interactive workshops of two days; six one-to-one coaching sessions; delivered virtually or in person over six months
Pricing	£64,000 for twenty participants

CASE STUDY: Targeted solution

The challenge

A global security company was facing underperformance across several teams, with noticeable leadership gaps and increasing attrition among high-potential staff. Managers lacked confidence in handling difficult conversations, aligning their teams to strategic goals and motivating individuals effectively.

The solution

We delivered the *Confident Leaders, Thriving Teams* programme with mid-level managers of identified teams. The programme was delivered over six months, combining diagnostics with targeted development:

- Strengths profiling and leadership competency assessments before and after the programme
- Three interactive workshops (two days each) focused on core leadership behaviours, team engagement and real-time problem solving
- Six individual coaching sessions per manager to embed learning and tackle specific leadership challenges

The results

- Measurable increase of 24% in leadership confidence and clarity as recognised by managers of participants
- Team engagement scores improved across all participating managers by 18%

- Staff turnover in affected teams reduced by 20% within twelve months of programme completion

---

What you will find is that the act of writing all of this down for each of your packages will bring you far more clarity in your conversations with corporate decision makers, giving them confidence in your credibility and, ultimately, trust in you.

What to standardise and what to customise for scalability

Every organisation likes to think that their particular business challenge is unique to them. It usually isn't. The challenge for you and I is how to balance efficiency with corporate-specific needs. Standardisation makes your business more scalable and profitable but customisation increases perceived value and client buy-in.

Elements to standardise in your corporate packages:

- Core methodology and process: Your proven approach should remain consistent across clients.

- Programme structure and deliverables: Keep foundational elements such as timelines, key outcomes and session structures the same.

- Pricing and engagement models: Avoid reinventing pricing for each client.

- Marketing and messaging: Standardise how you describe your services to maintain clarity and credibility.

For example, a six-month leadership development programme could have the same format of six workshops and one-to-one coaching, but the content within each module can be adapted for different industries.

Elements to customise in your corporate packages:

- Case studies and examples: Use industry-relevant examples to increase relatability.

- Company-specific challenges: Tweak discussions or frameworks to align with their internal goals.

- Implementation support: Offer tailored recommendations based on company size, culture or priorities.

- Delivery format: Some clients may prefer in-person sessions, while others will need virtual options.

For example, a three-month operational consulting engagement might follow a standard structure of stakeholder interviews, workflow analysis and a strategic recommendations report. That framework stays the same regardless of the client but what changes is the detail: the metrics you analyse, the case studies you use, the language you reflect back from the organisation and how the recommendations are prioritised based on their specific goals. One manufacturing client might focus on reducing downtime, while a professional services firm might prioritise cross-functional collaboration. The bones of the package stay the same but the wrapping is tailored to their world.

The way forward for a scalable yet flexible model is to offer a core package with modular elements that can be swapped out or adapted. We have a wide variety of topics we can cover in our leadership development programmes and I swap these in and out of the programme's core structure as I co-create the solution with the corporate decision maker and listen to their specific organisational challenges.

Think of your services as being like a restaurant menu. The core dishes, or core content and process, remain the same, but clients can choose from a selection of add-ons to meet their specific requirements.

A REAL EXAMPLE: Packages

Daniel (not his real name) is a communication skills trainer who works with mid-level managers to help them have clearer, more confident conversations, especially around feedback, delegation and influencing across the business. He knew his work was good – he had seen it land in the room – but he was struggling to convert that into consistent opportunities with corporate clients.

His signature programme at the time was a three-month communication skills programme – structured, well designed and full of practical content – but new clients weren't saying yes. He kept hearing versions of 'This looks great, but...'. Daniel was left wondering if his work just wasn't what corporates wanted, or if he was simply packaging it in the wrong way.

We took a step back and looked at the real issue: the ask was too big for a first engagement. The commitment, time, budget and buy-in felt risky for decision makers who didn't yet have a relationship with him. The content wasn't the problem, it was the structure.

We reworked his offer to make it easier for clients to say yes. His quick-win option became a series of three two-hour interactive sessions under the banner 'Say It So They Hear It'. Focused on practical tools for giving feedback that landed, the sessions were spaced over six weeks so participants had time to practise, reflect and build confidence in between. It was simple, focused and low-risk and it gave decision makers a chance to experience the impact of his work before committing to more.

With that in place, we then developed his signature programme into a six-month modular programme: 'Communicating with Impact'. It included quarterly diagnostics, a blend of virtual and in-person workshops, live practice labs and optional one-to-one coaching for key managers. This wasn't just a training series – it was designed to embed communication as a core management capability aligned with wider cultural goals like collaboration and accountability.

By offering two clearly structured packages, one for getting started (quick win) and one for deeper transformation (signature programme), Daniel made it easier for corporate clients to engage with him and scale the work over time. Just as importantly, the modular structure allowed for co-creation, making the programme feel tailored without needing to reinvent the wheel each time.

Daniel didn't need to change what he was great at, he just needed to shape it in a way that made it easy to say yes.

Pitfalls to avoid

When structuring your corporate service packages, it's easy to fall into common traps that can make your offerings less effective in delivering results. Avoiding these three pitfalls will ensure that your services are high-value and results-driven:

1. Not having or creating your own framework or model. One of the biggest traps coaches, consultants and trainers fall into is not having a clear proprietary framework. If your approach is indistinguishable from every other executive coach, HR consultant or sales trainer, corporate buyers will struggle to see why they should choose you over the competition. A unique framework or model gives your work structure, credibility and a distinct intellectual property edge. It transforms your expertise from a general

service into a proprietary solution, making it easier for decision makers to buy.

2. Being too conceptual and not focusing on practical, actionable results. Many experts make the mistake of being too theoretical in their content. Corporate clients don't invest in services just for interesting discussions – they invest for tangible results. If your programme is full of big ideas but lacks clear and effective action steps, participants will struggle to apply what they've learned, and decision makers may question the return on investment (ROI) of your service.

3. Covering too much ground instead of focusing on one clear, high-impact outcome. Another common mistake is trying to include too much information in a single package. There is depth to many of the topics we cover, but overwhelming participants with too much content dilutes effectiveness. Corporates don't need the full breadth of knowledge you have – they need a laser-focused solution to a specific challenge.

Your turn: Structuring your packages

Now it's your turn to shape what you offer so it's clear, structured and easy for corporate clients to buy. This is about drawing together what you already know works and presenting it in a way that helps decision makers see the value, fast. Use the prompts below to refine one or two core packages.

Develop the two levels of package you could offer

These should be a small, quick-win package that addresses the surface issue. For example, the equivalent of a two-day workshop delivered over a period of a couple of weeks on the topic of conflict to cooperation in teams for mid-level managers, and coaching a couple of leaders within the organisation with before and after assessments completed by them and their managers. Then a deeper, longer-term signature package addressing the fundamental issue. For example, a six-month programme including a full consulting process with one department.

For example, 'I can offer a focused solution for X or a deeper programme to address Y.'

Decide on your core delivery format

First think about the length: how long does it run? Then consider the format: will it be coaching, training, consulting or a blend? In person, virtual or online modules? Last, establish the structure: what are the key components or milestones?

Work out how you could make your solution easier to understand and buy

Is the name clear and outcome-focused? Is the structure clearly defined?

What is the core content and process? What content can you adapt / swap out when co-creating with the decision maker?

What are the key takeaways or impact? Quantify where you can.

Capture results delivered

Reflect on results you have delivered for clients to date. This can be work with small businesses or private clients, as well as any corporate clients. Think about the results in terms of outcomes that matter to corporates and quantify them where you can.

Take your answers and start shaping them into a one-pager or even just a few key talking points. You'll refine this as you go, but having a structured offer on paper gives you instant clarity – and that builds confidence, which will come through in every conversation you have.

Final thoughts: Make it easy for them to say yes

This step is where your expertise starts to translate into something tangible, useful and commercially compelling. When your packages are clear, structured and tied to positive outcomes, corporate decision makers quickly see your value, with conversations moving from interest to action more quickly. Proposals take less time to write and you stop reinventing the wheel every time someone shows interest. Remember: this is about helping organisations make confident decisions. The clearer your packages are, the easier it is for them to say yes and the more scalable your business becomes.

In this chapter, you've clarified what your packages are, so now let's talk about how to price them to reflect the value of your work and give you the confidence to charge what it's worth.

8
Step 3: Price

With your services positioned and packaged, the next step is one that many coaches, consultants and trainers find the most challenging – pricing. Pricing corporate services is different from pricing for individual clients. Many service providers undercharge, basing their pricing on time rather than value, or struggle with confidence when quoting fees. This chapter will help you develop a value-based pricing strategy that aligns with corporate expectations. It will help you create a clear and flexible pricing framework that suits different corporate budgets and build the confidence to charge what your services are truly worth.

Unlike individuals who pay for personal growth, corporates invest in business outcomes. You may think they are buying coaching, training or consulting services but they are actually buying:

- A solution to a business problem – for example, reducing talent attrition, increasing sales

- A measurable improvement in performance, engagement or profitability

- Risk reduction, ensuring their teams and leaders are equipped for success

If you price too low, organisations may assume you lack expertise or impact. Many organisations expect to pay premium rates for specialised expertise, and pricing too low can make them sceptical of your value. It also makes it difficult to grow your business and deliver quality work. Your pricing needs to reflect the business transformation and ROI you provide, not just the time you spend delivering services.

Value-based pricing instead of time-based pricing

One of the biggest mistakes I see people make is charging per hour, per session or per day. This is time-based pricing, and it reduces your value to the number of hours worked rather than the business impact you create. You are limiting your earning potential, because you are capping your income at how many hours you can work. Corporates are not paying for your time, they are paying for your expertise and results.

Instead of charging X for a package of so many sessions, frame your pricing based on the outcome first. For example:

- Time-based pricing: A package of six coaching sessions at £3,000

- Value-based pricing: £6,000 for a three-month leadership transformation programme designed to improve retention, engagement and leadership effectiveness by 20%. This includes:

  - Initial leadership assessment

  - Six coaching sessions

  - Mid-point review

  - Closing leadership assessment and review'

Corporate decision makers are comfortable with high-value investments as long as the return is clear.

Key components in pricing

When it comes to pricing your services, too many coaches, consultants and trainers either guess or base their fees on what others seem to be charging. A more sustainable approach is to understand the essential components that ensure your business is both profitable and predictable.

Set your baseline price

To ensure sustainability and profitability, set a baseline price, the minimum you will charge for your services. There are two main aspects to working this out:

1. **Understand your business costs.** I'm a great fan of the approach Michael Michalowicz outlines in his book *Profit First*.[13] He recommends that your business pays you first, then allocates money for profit, taxes and, lastly, expenses. There are some useful percentages he introduces as a benchmark for different revenue levels, ensuring that businesses allocate funds wisely and operate within sustainable margins. For example, he suggests that for businesses earning under US$250,000 in revenue, about 50% should go towards the owner's pay, 30% towards operating expenses, 15% towards taxes and 5% towards profit. These percentages shift as revenue grows, helping businesses maintain profitability while scaling.

2. **Make sure you factor in business development time.** When you start out in business, all of your time is spent on business development but this changes as you win work. As you spend more time on delivering to clients, it becomes increasingly important to maintain about one-third of your time on business development. This helps you avoid the common feast–famine

trap, where projects end and you have nothing lined up because business development was neglected. You want consistency in your business. What this means is that the number of days you are available to deliver to clients is going to be about one-third of the time you spend working in or on your business in total. That one-third has to cover your operating expenses, taxes, owner's pay and profit. With one-third spent on business development and one-third on delivery, the remaining one-third is for content creation, admin and your professional development.

The question is, how much do you want to be paid by your business each year?

Once you have that number – let's say it represents 50% of the overall revenue for your business – using Michael Michalowicz's numbers and the additions of 30% operating expenses, 15% taxes and 5% profit, calculate the total revenue your business needs.

Now work out how many days you want to work each year. After weekends and, say, ten public holidays, there are 251 work days in a year assuming you work five days a week. Take off holidays, let's say eight weeks, and now you are left with 211 days. Divide this by three for the number of client-facing or income-earning days, and you have roughly seventy days to earn all of the revenue for that year for your business.

Let's say you wanted to pay yourself £120,000 before tax. Using Michael Michalowicz's percentages, you would need a revenue of £240,000 in your business with just seventy days to earn this. Therefore, each day of client-facing work needs to bring in a minimum of roughly £3,430.

Develop a clear and flexible pricing framework

Your pricing needs to align with the structure of your packages and, as we have seen, in most cases that means having two clear options: a quick win and a signature programme.

These two tiers give corporate buyers the ability to choose based on their current needs, budget and level of readiness. More importantly, they help you position yourself as a provider with range, someone who can deliver immediate value and support longer-term transformation.

The table below shows how this can look in practice.

When talking with decision makers from not-for-profit organisations such as government agencies and charities, it is usual to offer reduced prices by as much as 15%–25%.

	Quick-win package	Signature programme
What is it?	This is a lower-commitment, high-impact engagement designed to solve a specific problem quickly.	This is your deeper, more transformational offer, typically delivered over several months and with a broader scope.
Examples	£8,000 for a two-day team communication workshop, including a short prep call and post-session summary £6,500 for a focused coaching sprint with two mid-level leaders over six weeks £7,200 for a departmental needs assessment and a brief recommendations report	£96,000 for a six-month leadership development programme for twenty managers, including workshops, diagnostics and one-to-one coaching £57,000 for a modular programme blending training and coaching to support managers through organisational change £62,000 for a consulting engagement that includes a full diagnostic, recommendations and implementation support across two departments
Benefits	These quick-win packages help open the door and they often lead to deeper engagements.	Each of these includes clear deliverables, timelines and measurable outcomes, which gives corporate decision makers the confidence they need to commit.

Benchmark against what corporates typically pay for

It is useful to have an idea of the rates corporates will typically pay. In my experience, an offer of six sessions of one hour each of executive coaching is typically £3,000–£8,000. If you are highly specialised with specific ROIs you can prove and also include assessments, this would be much higher.

A six-month leadership development programme for ten leaders is typically £36,000–£58,000. If you add in one-to-one coaching support or have larger numbers, this would be much higher – up to about £100,000.

Consultancy support pricing varies depending on the business results the client is looking for but could look like this:

- Needs assessment and diagnosis: £18,000–£32,000

- Strategic recommendations and roadmap: £30,000–£50,000

- Implementation and change management support: £50,000–£120,000

- Evaluation and ongoing advisory support: £20,000 upward

I find that corporate decision makers often have a number in mind that they are willing to consider. When flushing this out, I talk in terms of 'This would be in the ballpark of... how does that sound?' Then I say nothing until I see a reaction, or they respond. If they suggest this is a little high, I do not discount. Instead, I adjust the scope of work to fit their budget. For example, I might swap out one-to-one coaching for group coaching or reduce the hours of any individual advisory support.

If your pricing makes you slightly uncomfortable – note that I said 'slightly' – you're probably charging the right amount. Too much out of your comfort zone and decision makers will pick up on your unease, which will work against you.

How to overcome pricing anxiety

Reframe your price as an investment, not a cost. Corporates are receiving something of value – a business outcome – for their investment. If you don't have your own figures, use credible sources such as the International Coaching Federation (ICF), which found that companies investing in executive coaching realised an average ROI of up to seven times the coaching cost.[14] Intellek suggests a training ROI of at least 100%–200%, meaning a return of £2–£3 for every £1 invested in training through business impact.[15] Unfortunately, there is little ROI data for consulting, so it is even more important to start collecting your own.

Other ways to become more comfortable with pricing are to practise saying your prices out loud until they feel natural and to recognise that premium pricing attracts serious clients. Remember that corporate budgets are much larger than individual coaching/training budgets.

If there are specific charities and causes that you would love to support with your services, having a number of corporate clients who pay premium pricing enables you to provide your services to causes you love at heavily discounted prices.

A REAL EXAMPLE: Pricing

Let me introduce you to James (not his real name), a thoughtful and experienced sales consultant who came to me feeling quietly frustrated. He knew his work delivered results, as he'd helped client teams shorten sales cycles, close more enterprise deals and build genuine confidence in their sales approaches. When it came to pricing, however, he found himself guessing. He told me he'd just quoted £6,000 for a six-month B2B sales transformation programme. 'I picked a number that felt reasonable,' he admitted. There was no structure, no real logic, and underneath there was a familiar fear of *If I charge more, they might walk away.*

James isn't alone. Many brilliant consultants and coaches underprice themselves because they don't yet see their work through the lens of business value – they see it through delivery time or what they think the client will accept. This often results in incredible value delivered at a fraction of its worth and a model that's hard to sustain. We unpacked what James's programme did. It consistently shortened the sales cycle by two months and improved enterprise deal conversion. For one client alone, that translated into an estimated £250,000 in additional revenue over the next year. That figure changed everything.

We reframed James's offer around those outcomes, renamed it The Sales Acceleration Blueprint and introduced a new base price for the same programme of £25,000, reflecting a ten times ROI. What we did was align his price with the impact his work was already delivering. That same quarter, he landed a corporate client at £25,000, more than four times what he'd previously charged for the same work, simply packaged and priced differently. More than that, he felt confident presenting it. He was no longer hoping for buy-in; he was standing in the value of what he offered.

Pitfalls to avoid

These five common pricing mistakes can seriously undercut both your revenue and your credibility:

1. Pricing by the hour, day or session. Time-based pricing limits your earning potential and signals that what you offer is a commodity. Corporates don't buy time, they buy results. A flat fee tied to an outcome or business result makes it easier for

buyers to understand the investment and easier for you to scale your work.

2. Letting nerves dictate your number. Many coaches, consultants and trainers undercharge because quoting higher fees feels uncomfortable. This results in either resenting the engagement or struggling to grow because their margins are too tight. Remember: it's OK to feel slightly stretched when quoting your fee. That feeling of stretch represents growth.

3. Dropping your price too quickly. When a decision maker hesitates or says they don't have a budget, many service providers immediately offer a discount. Don't. Instead, adjust the scope. Suggest a scaled-back version that still delivers impact by swapping out the most expensive elements; for example, you could replace one-to-one coaching or individual support with group sessions. This maintains your credibility and avoids setting a precedent for discounting.

4. Not setting clear payment terms upfront. I learned this the hard way. I once agreed to partial payment upfront for a three-month programme, which then got extended to six months due to internal delays. The final payment didn't come through until month eight. Now I always ask for full payment upfront, no matter the length of the programme. It protects your cash flow and sets a professional tone from the outset.

5. Quoting per person instead of 'up to' a fixed number. This is another easy trap to fall into. I once priced for a group but also mentioned what it worked out at per participant. When fewer people enrolled than expected, the client insisted on paying the per-person rate, which left me significantly out of pocket because it meant my day rate dropped. Now I always quote a fixed price for 'up to fifteen people' or similar.

Here's an example of my client Peter, not his real name. Peter delivers leadership and team development programmes and was feeling good about a recent opportunity: a prospective client had shown strong interest in his three-month programme and was ready to discuss numbers. When Peter asked how many leaders they were thinking of putting through the programme, the client said seven. In the past, Peter might have quoted a per-person fee without realising the risks, but this time, he used a simple shift we'd discussed: pricing the programme as a package for 'up to ten participants'. He confidently shared the price range, explaining that the fee remained the same whether the client enrolled seven or ten leaders. The client didn't push back. Instead, he replied, 'I'll find three extra folks to put through the programme.' That one phrase 'up to ten' didn't just protect Peter's revenue. It brought him three additional participants making the delivery more efficient and the programme even more impactful. More importantly, it reinforced his position as a professional partner who knows how to structure offers in a way that's clear, scalable and commercial.

Small shift, big result: that's the power of pricing with clarity and confidence.

Your turn: Defining your value-based pricing strategy

Use the following prompts to develop a clear, confident pricing strategy for your corporate services that reflects the value you provide and aligns with corporate expectations, supporting sustainable business growth.

Know what measurable improvement your service creates

For example, in past projects you've been able to increase leadership retention by 20% or reduce the average sales cycle from six months to three months. If you don't know these numbers, start collecting this data and in the meantime use industry benchmarks from credible bodies such as ICF, Gartner, McKinsey etc.

Define the transformation and ROI for clients

Corporates expect an ROI, so define how your service delivers measurable impact. What key outcomes will it achieve? For example, improved leadership confidence, better team collaboration, process improvement, higher employee engagement.

Note: If you are struggling to answer these questions, go back through Step 1 and Step 2 in the previous two chapters. Reflect on clients you've previously worked with, and the impact and outcomes achieved.

Set your baseline price

Using the information outlined in this chapter, work out what your minimum acceptable price for your core service is. Consider your business expenses, taxes and profit, your time commitment and the going market rates covered in this chapter. You can also find updated rates using Google or AI. What price reflects the true value of your service, not just your time? Think about the ROI and transformation your service delivers.

Remember: if your price makes you feel slightly uncomfortable, you are probably charging the right amount.

Structure a flexible, value-based pricing model

Use the two-tier delivery model explained earlier to provide options. For each package level, quick win and signature, list the key deliverables and write down the investment figures. Practise swapping out more expensive elements such as one-to-one support for group support and calculating the new price. You want to be able to give a ballpark figure for a couple of options when in conversations with decision makers.

Build pricing confidence

How can you reframe pricing as an investment rather than a cost? An example might be: 'This programme will help your company save £100,000 in staff turnover costs.'

How will you handle objections without lowering your price? An example could be: 'I can adjust the scope to fit your budget while maintaining impact by swapping out, for example, individual coaching sessions/support for group coaching/facilitation.'

Own your pricing. The more confident you are, the more confident corporate clients will be in hiring you.

Final thoughts: Own the value you deliver

Pricing is often the biggest internal hurdle for coaches and consultants moving more fully into the corporate space and it's probably because the numbers represent your value, confidence and boundaries. When you price well you're seen as a serious, credible partner who can afford to deliver your best work. You get to build a sustainable, profitable business and create space to serve causes or clients you care about at reduced rates.

Remember that your fee is part of the message. Pricing low doesn't make you more appealing, it actually makes you less trusted. If you're still working on feeling confident quoting the numbers you've come up with here, that is normal. Confidence grows from clarity, repetition and evidence, just like any other attribute. This will help you shift from justifying your pricing to owning it.

This chapter has helped you get your pricing strategy in place; now it's time to build a list of right-fit organisations and corporate decision makers to connect with. In Step 4, we'll move into how to identify, research and qualify your ideal prospects before you even reach out.

9
Step 4: Prospect

In Step 1, you explored which industries or sectors are the best fit for you because they are grounded in your experience, interests and values. That gave you clarity on where to position yourself in the market. Here, we go a level deeper. We move from identifying the type of organisation to identifying specific companies and, from there, the decision makers inside them who are most likely to value your work.

This step isn't about outreach or starting conversations just yet, it's about focus and finding out:

- Which companies are a strong match for your positioning and offer the kind of challenges you're equipped to solve

- Who inside those companies is responsible for the outcomes your work supports

- How you can map this clearly so your business development efforts are targeted, not scattergun

Being selective at this stage saves you time, increases traction and sets the foundation for consistent opportunities. The goal here is to build a clear, considered list of potential organisations and key individuals so that in Step 5, where we focus on how to reach out in meaningful ways, you're already connected with the right people.

Prospecting matters. Many coaches, consultants and trainers make the mistake of jumping straight into outreach without a targeted prospect list. The problem is that you could be reaching out to people who can't approve budgets or don't need your expertise. You'll waste time and get frustrated with low response rates.

Corporates are complex and decision-making isn't always straightforward. Frequently, there are multiple people involved in the decision-making process, and some of them you will never get to meet. The people you do engage with may be among the following:

- True economic decision makers – the people who approve budgets and make final purchasing decisions

- Decision influencers – those who influence the decision maker but don't hold budget authority (for example, HR business partners, heads of learning and development, other department heads)

- Gatekeepers – assistants or lower-level managers who screen requests before they reach the decision maker

Your job is to find and focus on the real decision makers. The more qualified your prospect list, the easier your outreach in Step 5 will be. A smaller, well-researched prospect list is far more effective than a long, random list of contacts.

Key elements of prospecting

Effective prospecting is about relevance and intentionality. Here are the seven elements to get right when identifying the organisations and individuals who are most likely to value your work:

1. Move from industry to organisation

In Step 1, you reflected on the industries and sectors that best align with your experience, interests and values. Now it's time to zoom in. Which specific organisations in those sectors are doing interesting work, going through change or facing the kinds of challenges you're equipped to help with?

Start noticing which companies are hiring, merging, rebranding, restructuring or expanding, as these can all be signs of momentum and need. Tools like Google Alerts or AI can help you track what's happening in the sectors you serve.

2. Find the optimum organisation size

Over the past twenty years of selling my company's services to corporates, I've found that there is a sweet spot in terms of organisation size. Those with 500–5,000 employees tend to make quicker decisions and there aren't as many layers of bureaucracy involved in the process. Even better are those going through growth and experiencing the growing pains of expansion, scaling leadership and maintaining company culture amid rapid change. These organisations are actively looking for structured leadership development, culture transformation and performance solutions to support their next phase. For example, one of our telecoms clients, who we've worked with for more than twelve years, started with a conversation where they explained that they were implementing a management competency framework and wanted a suite of leadership development qualifications that were practical and relevant and fitted with their framework. They had an immediate need and we could respond quickly and flexibly to meet that need.

On the one hand, larger organisations (10,000+ employees) often have bigger budgets but the decision-making process can be longer and more complex, requiring multiple approvals across departments. If you are choosing global organisations to work with, looking at regional offices or country-specific divisions can often be a faster route to securing work than trying to engage at the global HQ level. Regional decision makers typically have more autonomy over budgets and specific challenges that require tailored solutions, making it easier to gain traction and move forward with a proposal. For example, a global energy company, another of our clients, recognised that they had a number of senior leaders who were coming up to retirement and they were keen to ensure their rich expertise and experience was passed down to the next generation of leaders. The challenge for them was that the regions they operate in are huge and have different requirements in terms of culture and understanding. We partnered with their MEENAA region – the Middle East, East and North Africa, Asia and Australasia – and provided mentoring programmes for their leaders in different forms.

On the other hand, smaller companies (under 500 employees) may be more flexible but often have tighter budgets or a preference for internal solutions. The exception to this are high-growth start-ups such as software and technology companies, where there are small numbers of employees but an expectation of huge growth and budgets to match. For example, a marketing company that provides a digital platform is currently one of our clients and is undergoing a lot of change after new owners stepped in. Things change quickly in this organisation, and we have been able to flex and adapt with their needs. With these sorts of clients, it's worth considering being paid upfront, as often there's a rush to get started and then some delays in continuing programmes as things shift and change in the organisation.

Don't rule out organisations with fewer than 500 employees or the big whales with 10,000+ employees. There will always be exceptions to the rule. We've worked with organisations of just a few hundred employees that turned out to be dream clients both in terms of the experience of working with them and the financial return. We've also worked with many organisations that have more than 10,000 employees and operate globally. Some of these have become long-standing clients of more than a decade. It's less about size on paper and more about alignment and need.

3. Remember that the gold is in your network

Many coaches and consultants immediately start cold prospecting when looking for corporate clients, ignoring the people they already know who could help them secure opportunities. I get it. The thought of having a conversation about who they could introduce you to feels salesy. There is a better way to reach out to them, but before we explore strategies to do this in Step 5, come up with a list of those people in your network. Think about:

- Former colleagues and managers – they may now be in decision-making roles or possibly have connections who are

- Past corporate prospects – even if they didn't buy from you before, circumstances may have changed

- Industry contacts – people you've met at conferences, networking events or on LinkedIn

- Friends and family in corporate roles – they might introduce you to decision makers in their company

- Your alumni network – many universities and professional associations offer corporate networking opportunities

Remember: it's not always about who you know, it's about who they know. Just one introduction can lead to multiple corporate contracts.

4. Identify who the right corporate decision makers are for you

Identifying the right decision maker depends on who buys your type of service. In the table below are some of the most common decision makers based on the service you provide.

Service type	Key decision maker
Management and leadership development	Chief HR officers (CHROs), learning and development directors
Executive coaching	COOs, CEOs, senior HR executives, CHROs
Sales and performance coaching	Sales directors, commercial directors
Post-merger consulting	Chief transformation officers, COOs

Not everyone you talk to will be a true economic decision maker. You will come across HR generalists and mid-level managers who may be interested and influence decisions but lack the power to make those decisions. Junior employees in the right department might connect you with the right person but can't make buying decisions.

Assistants and gatekeepers will filter information and may block your access to the decision maker, but treat them well because they can be powerful allies in reaching decision makers. For example, I wanted to work with a particular oil and gas company and managed to get hold of the contact details for the CHRO's assistant. She was polite, and I made sure that my first conversation was designed to find out more information rather than push for a meeting with the CHRO. After a couple of calls of this nature, we had built a connection and rapport. It was only on my next call, after establishing a relationship with her, that I explained more about some of the organisations we were working with and the types of problems we were helping them solve. She immediately said, 'Nicky, we need to get you in a meeting with our CHRO,' and promptly gave me a few dates and times when he was available. The first thing the CHRO asked when we got to meet was, 'I want to know how you managed to get this meeting with me.' I blushed and said 'persistence'. Fortunately, he laughed and yes, we went on to work with his company for a number of years.

Always aim for the highest-level person who is responsible for the budget and strategy in your service area, or who has line of sight of the problem you help solve. Treat people well no matter what level they are, because you never know where a conversation may take you.

5. Know where to find the right decision makers

Once you know which organisations and roles you want to engage with, the next step is finding their contact details. One of the best sources for finding corporate decision makers is LinkedIn. Here, you can search by job title and country without having to have a Premium account or Sales Navigator. Having Sales Navigator, however, does make the process significantly easier, especially when you need to reach out to third-tier connections (people outside your immediate network).

If I want to connect with the decision maker on LinkedIn, frequently I will just request to connect and send no note. I find that many people will simply accept my connection request. Even if you don't have a Premium LinkedIn account with access to Sales Navigator, start by connecting with people in your industry to expand your first-degree network. The larger your network, the easier it is to reach relevant corporate decision makers.

6. Create a qualified prospect list

What we are doing here is building a high-quality prospect list rather than randomly reaching out to hundreds of people. Strong prospects look like this:

- They have decision-making authority and can approve budgets and strategy.

- Their organisation fits your ideal client profile in terms of size, industry and need.

- They have business challenges that align with your services.

- They allocate a budget for your specific services.

Based on what you've uncovered, start building a working list of twenty to thirty organisations that align with your positioning. Write down the names of one or two decision makers per organisation (ideally with LinkedIn profiles or direct contact info) and make notes on why each organisation is a fit (growth, change, industry alignment etc).

Don't aim for perfection, because this list will evolve and it's much easier to refine and deepen once you've set it up. Consider using a customer relationship management (CRM) platform such as HubSpot, which has a free version.

7. Work your list

It's not enough to build the list – you have to use it and refine it. Set aside regular time each week, even just thirty minutes, to keep your prospecting active. This might mean updating company info, refining your notes, watching for leadership changes or preparing tailored insights to share later on. Your prospect list is a living tool that evolves with your focus, your offers and your conversations.

The clearer your prospecting, the more confident your outreach will feel and the stronger your results in Step 5 will be.

A REAL EXAMPLE: Prospecting

Let me tell you about Marie (not her real name), a consultant specialising in team dynamics. She joined my programme frustrated by months of unresponsive outreach. She'd been sending thoughtful messages to mid-level HR professionals but hearing nothing back.

She told me, 'I know I could help, but it's like shouting into the void.' We looked at her background and realised she had fifteen years of experience in professional services but she hadn't approached a single prospect in that sector. She was also focusing on the wrong level of contact: mid-level managers who are decision influencers rather than decision makers.

We used her past experience to build a list of mid-sized professional services firms that were scaling rapidly, then zeroed in on HR directors and COOs, people who were more likely to be grappling with culture and retention challenges. She also reached out to her former colleagues, one of whom introduced her to a CHRO actively looking for a solution to poor collaboration across remote teams. That introduction led to a two-day workshop which then grew into a six-month engagement and a second programme for the senior leadership team – all from refocusing her prospecting efforts and leaning into her existing credibility.

The shift? She stopped chasing cold leads and started aligning her prospecting with her background, values and network. That's when things clicked.

Pitfalls to avoid

Even experienced experts can fall into these traps. Here's what to watch out for:

1. Creating a prospect list based on hope, not fit. Many people build a list based on brand recognition ('I'd love to work with Google') rather

than organisational fit. Big names are tempting, but working with them can often be a long, drawn-out bureaucratic process. Include a few big names if you want to, but make sure you have plenty of smaller or regional hubs on your list too.

2. Ignoring where they live and the organisations around them. There's something comforting about knowing you are just around the corner or you pass by the organisation's offices on your way to taking your kids to school. You want to leverage this proximity.

3. Rushing to outreach without doing your homework. Prospecting is not just list-building, it's research. When you don't take time to understand the company's size, industry and challenges, your outreach becomes vague and ineffective. A smaller list of well-researched, high-quality prospects beats a spreadsheet of 500 cold names every time.

4. Confusing decision influencers with decision makers. It's tempting to celebrate when someone in HR gets excited about your offerings, but if they don't control the budget, it may not go anywhere. Always ask yourself: 'Is this a decision maker or a decision influencer?' Remember to be gracious with influencers and gatekeepers but aim your strategy at those with decision-making power.

Your turn: Creating your qualified prospect list

Let's start to build your qualified prospect list, not a vague wish list, but a clear, focused set of potential organisations and decision makers that align with your positioning.

Define your ideal corporate client

You've already done the groundwork in Step 1, where you reflected on the industries and sectors most aligned with your experience, interests and values. Now narrow the lens a little further by answering the following questions:

- Industry: Which industries are most likely to face the challenges you solve and align with your experience?

- Organisation size: What size of organisation typically has the need and budget for your services? For example, mid-sized (500–10,000), large (10,000+) or high-growth smaller firms with complex challenges.

- Common business challenges: What are the specific people, performance or process challenges these companies face that your solution directly addresses?

- Who feels the pain of the problem? It's not always HR. Consider directors of operations, COOs, department heads or business unit leaders – whoever has a line of sight on the issue you help solve. Make a list of likely decision maker roles.

Research your prospects

Now it's time to find examples that fit this profile. Start with LinkedIn and search by job title, company and location. Look at company websites and press releases. You don't need deep research yet, but you do need enough to understand why they might be a good fit.

Make notes on the following aspects: organisation, industry, company size, potential business need (recent changes or challenges, for example, growth, restructure, new leadership), decision maker's name, job title, whether you're connected on LinkedIn and why this company? (For example, shared values, interesting work, aligned with your expertise.)

Build your qualified prospect list

You can track your list using a CRM platform like HubSpot (the free version works well), a spreadsheet or even a notebook. Here's an example of a simple table you can use to get started.

Organisation	Blue Jay	Gold Finch
Industry	Telecoms	Insurance
Decision maker	Jane Doe	Jack Black
Job title	CHRO	VP of sales
Potential business need	Leadership retention	Sales team underperforming
Source (LinkedIn, website, event, etc)	LinkedIn	Website
Connected on LinkedIn?	N	Y
Next action step	Connect on LinkedIn	Contact

Aim to complete the table for at least twenty-five high-quality prospects and include relevant decision makers who are already in your network before moving on to Step 5.

Final thoughts: Prospecting is a strategic investment

This chapter has shown you that prospecting isn't about scattering seeds and hoping something grows – it's about planting with intention. When you take the time to build a well-researched prospect list, you set yourself up for warmer conversations, deeper trust and a far higher return on effort.

Prospecting done right isn't draining, it's energising. It helps you connect the dots between your expertise and the people who truly need it, and it builds momentum that will carry you through the sales process with more clarity and confidence.

This is the bridge between your value and their need, so let's now cross it together in Step 5, where we'll explore how to reach out and start meaningful, human-centred conversations with the decision makers you've identified without feeling salesy and in meaningful, low-pressure ways that build trust and open doors.

10
Step 5: Promote

By now you will have well-defined positioning, a clear service offering, a structured pricing strategy and a qualified prospect list of corporate decision makers. The challenge now is getting into meaningful conversations with them without feeling like you are pushing your services in an uncomfortable, salesy way. Unlike small business owners, corporate decision makers do not go to networking events hoping to meet service providers. They are busy focusing on business priorities and they don't want to be sold to. This is why traditional sales approaches often feel unnatural – because they don't match how corporate clients buy services. Instead of trying to sell your way in, you need to create the spaces where these conversations can happen naturally.

This chapter introduces the following three human-centred, non-salesy strategies to connect with decision makers in a way that feels good for both you and them:

1. Leveraging your existing network by asking for feedback, which often leads to referrals

2. Insight mining – taking on the role of a researcher gathering industry insights

3. Facilitating executive round tables – bringing decision makers together for peer-to-peer discussions

These three strategies are about building trust and naturally establishing yourself as an expert who understands the decision maker's world and their challenges. Remember: you don't have to do all three at once.

Corporate clients don't like hard sales tactics; they buy based on credibility, trust and demonstrated expertise. The more they see you facilitating insight-ful conversations, leading discussions on industry challenges and engaging with them and their peers in meaningful ways, the more they associate you with value, expertise and problem-solving capabilities.

Coaches, consultants and trainers often rely on one-off outreach tactics with corporate decision makers: ran-dom emails, cold LinkedIn messages or waiting for referrals. This makes it difficult to create consistent opportunities. The strategies outlined here are not just strategies – they are reproducible systems that, when applied consistently, have the ability to generate ongoing corporate opportunities. They allow you to make your expertise visible and valuable without sounding salesy, create a steady pipeline of conversations with decision makers who need your expertise, and build a trusted network of corporate leaders who see you as a valuable resource.

The three key strategies

Two of these strategies come from the Big 5 consultancy firms: McKinsey, Boston Consulting Group, Deloitte, PricewaterhouseCoopers and Ernst & Young. They use the exact same methods of insights-driven conversations and executive round tables to win multimillion-pound corporate contracts. Why wouldn't you do the same? If these methods work for the world's largest consultancies, they will work for you too on a scale that fits your business. When used consistently, these approaches not only bring in corporate clients but also establish you as the go-to expert in your industry.

Before we dive into these two strategies, let's not ignore your existing network.

1. Leveraging your existing network

One of the biggest mistakes people make when trying to sell to corporates is ignoring the network they already have. Instead, they jump straight into cold outreach, trying to convince strangers of their value. The reality is that someone you already know probably knows someone in a corporate decision-making role, but how do you reach out to your network without it feeling salesy? You ask for feedback – feedback on your package ideas and the sorts of problems and challenges you help solve. This allows the conversation to be genuine, natural and non-transactional while still opening the door to opportunities. To do this, follow these steps:

1. Identify people in your network who work in corporate roles, even if they are not direct decision makers, who are past colleagues, clients or industry connections and who are in professional associations or alumni groups.

2. Reach out with something like this: 'Hey Jo, I'm developing a new approach to [leadership development, sales training, HR consultancy etc] for [type of organisation] and would love your feedback. Would you be open to a quick chat?' Be willing to listen; you'll probably learn a lot from their feedback alone.

3. During the conversation, listen for signals such as 'Oh, we actually have that issue in our company' and 'You should speak to our HR department, we're struggling with...'.

4. If they mention a relevant opportunity, ask if they would be open to making an introduction. Many will, some won't, and that is perfectly OK. If they are, ask if they would be willing to introduce you via a three-way email or LinkedIn message. If they are not, thank them and ask how the problem shows up in their organisation – you'll learn a lot about the language to use with other corporate decision makers moving forward. Either way, thank them for their feedback and comment on how useful it has been.

This strategy works because there is no pressure and it is a genuine conversation. Also, people love to give feedback: they get to share their insights and feel helpful. It often leads to introductions because people naturally think of ways to help.

When I walk coaches, consultants and trainers through this strategy and get them to take action in real time, the results are amazing. Frequently, they are invited to have follow-up conversations or are introduced to relevant decision makers and end up securing work, speaking engagements and other opportunities. Never underestimate the power of simply asking for feedback.

2. Insight mining

This strategy is perfect for new LinkedIn connections and your existing network because it allows you to engage with them without pitching. Instead, you establish yourself as someone gathering industry insights, which decision makers are often happy to contribute to, and you will, in turn, learn a great deal about the business challenges you help with.

The secret to success with this strategy is choosing the right hot topic that engages corporate decision makers of a specific industry that aligns with a service you provide.

Current hot topics could include retaining your future leaders while facing aggressive competition for top talent in [specific industry], risk-taking and adaptability factors in leaders of fast-growing [specific industry] companies, or enhancing engagement, collaboration and development for distributed teams across multiple locations in [specific industry].

You want to interview ten to twelve relevant decision makers in the same industry, same type of organisation or same size of organisation.

Come up with four or five questions related to your topic and include these two additional questions: 'Are there one or two of your colleagues who I should be talking to about this insights paper?' (great for strategic introductions) and 'Is there anything else I should have asked you but didn't?' (great for uncovering insights that weren't even on your radar).

Now that you are ready to use insight mining to start conversations, follow these steps:

1. After connecting with relevant decision makers on LinkedIn, send a message similar to this: 'I'm speaking with HR leaders in the biotech sector about the challenge of retaining future leaders while facing aggressive competition for top talent. Would you be open to a quick fifteen-minute interview? I would love to include your perspective.' You can also send a version of this via email to corporate decision makers you have recently connected with.

2. Book a fifteen- to twenty-minute conversation over the phone, Teams or Zoom. You can do this in person but I would suggest booking more time for that because you will get into a longer conversation.

3. Ask if you can record the conversation for your purposes only, to help you with taking notes. It's important to stress that nobody else will listen to the recording and it will be erased once you have made detailed notes. Don't ask if you can record it ahead of time; this often leads into a discussion about who they need to get permission from. Make it a natural part of the

process in the moment. Ask your questions and get curious about their answers to delve deeper and get to insights.

4. Repeat with ten to twelve decision makers. Manage expectations and mention that you will circle back with your findings and insights and give them a sense of the deadline. You want them to be expecting a follow-up call from you not further than a month away to keep that connection going.

5. Go through the transcriptions or use AI to pull out five key insights and three surprises. You want these to circle back round to those you interviewed in your follow-up calls and also use these points when developing your insights paper.

6. Follow up with those you interviewed and share your insights. Ask them for feedback and be curious about what did and did not surprise them. Weave in the idea that these are the various issues you help organisations with, and look for an opening to transition the conversation into how you may be able to help them.

7. Write a two-page (two sides of A4) insights paper that you can email to those interviewed. Repurpose all of the material in your marketing: LinkedIn, your website, conference presentations, organisations' leadership teams, executive round tables and executive forums that you organise (more on this below).

This strategy works because you are building rapport with decision makers in a natural way, and people love sharing their expertise. It also positions you as an industry expert without selling and if there's an immediate need, they'll often ask about your work themselves.

For example, one of my clients, Carole, not her real name, moved countries and didn't know anyone in her new home. She used insight mining to broaden her network and become known. It didn't just broaden her network. The interview process and sharing insights in the follow-up conversations led to strong relationships, new clients and delivering programmes which addressed key identified challenges.

If you are wondering how you transition from a follow-up conversation to a sale, I'll cover that later in this chapter.

3. Executive round tables

The Big 5 consultancy companies, and others, use this strategy a lot. An executive round table is a small, invite-only discussion for corporate leaders in a specific industry. You are the organiser and instead of being seen as a service provider, you become the facilitator of a valuable conversation.

Similar to insight mining, you want to identify the right hot topic for your audience. You can also use the same topic as you use for insight mining, sharing your findings and insights to set the scene and kick-start the conversation at the beginning of the session. Once you have identified the hot topic and industry, you are ready to reach out to corporate decision makers and invite them to your round table by following these steps:

1. Reach out to about twenty-five decision makers in the same or related industries, inviting them to an executive round table on your identified hot topic. They can be a mix of people in your network and those who you have newly connected with on LinkedIn. You are aiming for about eight to attend. You can use LinkedIn Messaging or emails to invite them to an executive round table described as an intimate discussion with their peers, facilitated by you, focused on a timely and relevant topic. It can be virtual or in person. Virtual will probably be a sixty- to ninety-minute session, whereas for in person you want to allow time for networking and refreshments, so it will be closer to two hours.

2. Structure the session to include a short presentation to set the scene in the form of a guided discussion on the topic with questions you have prepared. Make sure you gently seed the fact that you help corporate clients with these issues and explain that you will follow up with each person after the session. You want to facilitate

the event professionally, keeping it focused on insights rather than it becoming a sales pitch.

3. Conclude the session by asking for key takeaways and make a note of these. Where possible, get permission at the start to record the conversation to make it easier in terms of note-taking.

4. Follow up with each participant with a conversation based on some of the things they mentioned in the discussion. Make sure to ask them if there was anything else they would like to share that they didn't want to in front of the group. Talk through some ideas you have on any challenges they are currently facing in the organisation. They will often open up more fully to you now that they see you as credible and there exists some trust between you.

This strategy works because you have positioned yourself as a strategic connector rather than a seller. Decision makers value conversations with their peers, as it can be lonely at the top. They are also curious about how others are handling similar issues to the ones they are facing. They will see you as the trusted expert you are in bringing them together and skilfully facilitating the discussions.

For example, one of my clients, Paul, was keen to systemise his lead generation with corporates and decided to prioritise executive round-table discussions. At first, it felt like a stretch. Hosting felt vulnerable but he committed to the process. He followed up with thoughtful, one-to-one conversations after each session. That's when things started to shift. Not only did he create genuine engagement, but he also began to build trust. Now he's celebrating new contracts won with more in the pipeline, all directly connected to those round tables. It's not just that he got results. It's that he built a system he can trust.

The fortune is in the follow-up

This is often the moment when doubts creep in, when it can feel awkward to shift from a helpful conversation to something that might lead to a sale. That's normal, but it's also when the opportunity really opens up. You've already invested in building trust, you've listened deeply, you've understood their world, and you've shared meaningful insights. Now it's simply about extending that same curiosity a little further, gently exploring whether this is something they'd like to move forward with and if your support could make a difference. You're not 'selling at' them – you're standing alongside them, helping them see a roadmap forward.

A simple way to do this is to ask open, reflective questions like 'Is this something you're already addressing internally?' or 'Would it be helpful to explore some ways you could tackle this?' This creates a natural opening to talk about solutions without feeling pushy. You might also reflect back what you've heard and offer your perspective: 'It sounds like this is a priority area, especially with X and Y happening, would it be useful if I shared how I've supported other teams with something similar?'

This is where all the work you've done on positioning, packaging and pricing comes together. It allows you to hold the conversation with confidence, knowing you have something valuable to offer. When they start to lean in and ask, 'What would working together look like?', you're ready to co-create a solution that feels useful to them and aligned for you. It's about partnership, helping them take meaningful next steps towards the outcomes they care about.

A REAL EXAMPLE: Promoting

Diane (not her real name) is a coach and consultant who supports HR leaders in building more inclusive and connected cultures. When we started working together on Step 5 of the CSP, she was feeling stuck. Her promotional efforts were mostly passive: waiting to be invited in, hoping her content would be noticed and worrying that being more visible might come across as pushy or self-serving. She wasn't short on experience but she didn't yet have a way of sharing that value that felt natural to her. When we explored a more strategic, relationship-led approach, Diane decided to host an executive round table for HR decision makers.

At first, the idea felt uncomfortable, not because Diane didn't have the skills to facilitate it – far from it – but because she hadn't done anything like this before. She worried that people would turn her down or not turn up. She even worried that if they did turn up, she would do a poor job of facilitating.

She moved forward anyway, designing a focused conversation that brought together people from her network and others she genuinely wanted to build relationships with around a specific hot topic. It was about connection, insight and creating a space where senior leaders could speak openly with peers. The round table itself showcased Diane as a thoughtful and credible presence, someone who 'got it' without trying to sell anything, but the real value came in the follow-up.

By reconnecting one-to-one with each attendee, Diane uncovered three opportunities:

1. An invitation to speak on stage as part of a panel alongside senior leaders from global well-known companies.

2. A request to support an HR team navigating organisational change.

3. A coaching engagement with one of the attendees who resonated with Diane's approach and wanted to work with her directly.

   All of this came from one carefully curated conversation and a series of meaningful follow-ups. Diane was visible in a way that felt aligned, credible and deeply human, tapping into skills she already had.

Pitfalls to avoid

Even with great strategies, it's easy to stumble if you're not aware of the common missteps. Here are four that I see time and time again, even among experienced professionals:

1. Mistaking visibility for connection. Just because you're active on LinkedIn doesn't mean you're building relationships. Liking, posting and sharing can build awareness, but they rarely lead to conversations unless you have a strategy behind that approach. Use visibility as the starting point but make sure it leads to a meaningful conversation by using one of the strategies outlined above.

2. Defaulting to cold outreach too soon. There's a temptation to jump straight into messaging strangers and ignoring your wonderful network. Somehow it seems easier to reach out cold, but maybe that's because we tend to be less worried about the rejection of strangers than those we know. You want to start with your network first. They already know, like and trust you, and many of them would probably love to help. Ignore that inner voice that starts with 'What if...'.

3. Treating strategies as one-offs. Running one executive round table or sending out a few insights mining messages might spark interest but one-off efforts rarely lead to consistent results.

The power comes from repeatability, so turn your outreach into a rhythm that decision makers come to expect. Whether it's monthly or quarterly, consistency will consolidate your impact.

4. Choosing the wrong hot topic. You want something that is hot today, has a sense of urgency about it and aligns with a solution you have. If it doesn't resonate with corporate decision makers, they won't turn up. On the flip side, I've seen coaches and consultants go down rabbit holes that are interesting but do not align with their solutions or skill sets. Remember that this is part of your business development process, so make sure it's highly relevant to decision makers and in alignment with your solutions.

Your turn: Planning your own outreach

This step is all about creating conversations that build trust and open doors, not chasing leads or posting forever on LinkedIn. You now have three practical ways to increase visibility and create opportunities, so let's plan your outreach.

Start with your network

Before trying to engage new contacts, start with people who already know, like and trust you. Pick three to five people from your network; for example, past colleagues, LinkedIn connections, former clients or friends in corporate roles. Reach out using this simple message: 'Hey [Name], I'm developing a new approach to [leadership development/sales training/ HR consultancy] for [industry] and would love your feedback. I'm just keen to hear your thoughts. Would you be open to a quick chat?'

That's it. No pitch, no pressure, just a genuine conversation. Here's the key: listen well. If an opportunity emerges, simply ask: 'Would you be open to introducing me?' This one conversation can do more than a month of content ever will.

Choose a strategy to expand your reach

Next, pick one of the engagement strategies listed above to explore further, depending on which feels most appropriate for you.

Map your outreach plan

Use the prompts below to bring your chosen strategy to life:

- Hot topic: What's a timely challenge or issue you want to explore – one that links clearly to your services?
- Industry focus: Which industry or sector will you start with?

- How many people? How many conversations or participants are you aiming for?

- Who are they? You will probably need to reach out to twenty-five decision makers, a mix of people you know and those who are new to you, to get eight people attending an executive round table or ten to twelve decision makers for insight mining interviews. Work out who those twenty-five decision makers are, using your list from Step 4.

- Time frame: What's your time frame for outreach and follow-up?

- What does success look like? Is it five meaningful conversations, ten key insights, one new opportunity?

Draft your first message

Choose your strategy and write your first message to a decision maker. Keep it short, respectful and focused on value.

Final thoughts: Promoting your services through value-led experiences

All of the above strategies work well because you are offering something of value for the corporate decision maker before you get into a sales conversation. Instead of chasing clients, you are inviting them into discussions that are high-value for them. Your follow-up conversations are facilitated in a way that builds trust, not pressure. The best part about all of these strategies is that they don't have to be just one-time events. You can make them into a repeatable, systemised part of your business development strategy. Whether you host one every quarter, every other month or once a month, you are building a rhythm of engaging decision makers while naturally positioning yourself as an expert and seeding future client work.

Global consultancies regularly use these strategies of insight interviews and executive round tables. It's part of how they create thought leadership, connect with C-suite clients and shape demand for their services, and there's no reason you can't do the same, at your pace, with your voice and your impact.

This chapter has given you the tools to position yourself clearly, package your services in a corporate-friendly way, price confidently, build a qualified list of decision makers and engage them in a meaningful way.

Your roadmap to consistent corporate clients

You've now worked your way through the five essential steps of the CSP: Position, Package, Price, Prospect and Promote. Each step gives you a clear focus for how to be known for solving valuable, meaningful problems, how to shape your services so corporates want to buy them, how to price with confidence, how to connect with the right decision makers and how to build relationships that position you as a trusted, strategic partner.

Step	Focus	Key point
Step 1: Position	Clarify what you want to be known for	Align your business with the work that energises you and solves a clear business problem for a specific type of client. Strong positioning helps you attract the right opportunities and be seen as credible and relevant.
Step 2: Package	Make your services easy to buy	Shape your expertise into structured, outcome-focused offers that match how corporates buy. Start with two tiers: a quick-win option and a signature programme. Clear packaging builds confidence and trust.
Step 3: Price	Align fees with business value	Stop selling time. Price your offers based on the results they deliver and the scale of the problem they solve. A clear, consistent pricing model helps you get paid well and negotiate with confidence.
Step 4: Prospect	Identify the right organisations and people	Move from industries and sectors to specific companies and individual decision makers. Build a qualified prospect list so you're engaging with people who are most likely to value your work.
Step 5: Promote	Build visibility, trust and influence	Use low-pressure, relationship-first strategies like reactivating your network, insight mining or executive round tables to create meaningful conversations that open doors.

It's a lot to take in and if you're feeling a little overwhelmed, that's normal. You are shifting the foundations of how you think about your business and the clients you serve, not simply tweaking tactics. This takes time and it takes focus. Right now, it's easy to feel pulled in several directions wondering where to start, but progress doesn't come from trying to change everything at once. It comes from identifying the single biggest barrier holding you back and putting your energy into overcoming that first.

Let's simplify it.

Where's your biggest opportunity to create momentum?

Do you need:

- Sharper positioning so decision makers quickly grasp the value you bring?

- A clearer package that makes it easier for corporates to say yes?

- A more confident pricing strategy that reflects the real value of your work?

- Professional connections with decision makers who have the authority to bring you in?

- More consistent promotion so you stay front-of-mind with the right decision makers?

The Corporate Success Scorecard will help you get clear on this. It only takes five minutes and gives you a straight-forward snapshot of where your time and energy will have the most impact so you can make focused progress without getting pulled in too many directions.

Take the scorecard here:

https://corporatesuccess.scoreapp.com.

If that even feels like a bit much today, take a moment, step back, and ask yourself: 'What's one thing I can move forward with right now?' One simple shift. One clear decision. One small step that feels manageable. Progress doesn't come from tackling everything at once – it comes from small, steady actions that build over time. It's about creating a steady rhythm that creates stronger client relationships and a more predictable pipeline.

In Part Three, we'll focus on building steady momentum in a way that feels natural, sustainable and aligned with the kind of business you want to grow.

Let's move into making it real.

PART THREE
MAKING IT REAL

You've seen the map that will guide you to winning corporate clients on a consistent basis and you understand the shift needed from selling your skill set to solving meaningful problems and challenges organisations face. Instead of chasing, you are now building trust and influence, stepping into your authority and owning your space. You've probably had a few light-bulb moments about what is possible for you in the corporate space. Now it is time to bring all that insight down to earth, because knowing the pathway and walking it are two different things.

This part of the book is all about walking the pathway in a way that works with who you are. It takes courage to step forward, especially when the steps feel unfamiliar, but this is how we build confidence – by taking action. You are not expected to have it all figured out. Just begin. Expect and allow it to be imperfect and grow from there.

You might still have doubts: *Am I really ready?*, *What if I mess this up?*, *What if I still get ignored?* You are not alone in feeling this way. Many brilliant coaches, consultants and trainers start with the same worries and concerns. I know you can do this and in a way that is aligned with who you are. You don't need to become some super sales person or anyone else to succeed. You've been given clear steps and now you just need encouragement and a willingness to take these five steps of the CSP.

Now is the time when we turn ideas into actions. In this part of the book, you will find reassurance, practical guidance and a nudge or two to help you move forward from inspiration to implementation. Whether you are at the starting line or already taking your first steps, this part is designed to help you make it real, with momentum and the kind of support that means you are not doing this alone.

Inside this part of the book, you will find tools to help you start where you are, hear more real-life examples from people who have walked this path ahead of you and get the encouragement you are looking for to keep going even when things feel uncertain. I see this journey you are on as being about not just consistently landing corporate clients. It's about stepping into the kind of business you truly want to build to make the impact you want to have.

11
You're Not Alone

Before we go any further, I want to share a bit of my own journey into corporate work to show you that progress is rarely linear. Not to hold it up as the blueprint, but to show you what's possible when you take imperfect action and keep going, even when you don't feel ready. My path wasn't smooth or glamorous. In fact, it was full of doubts, detours and moments when I questioned whether I was good enough to win consistent corporate clients. If you're wrestling with similar thoughts, you're not alone.

My first steps into the corporate space

When I first broke into the corporate space, it was anything but smooth. Coming out of the NHS in the

UK, I'd never been taught marketing or selling. These words weren't even part of my vocabulary. What helped me take the first step was realising I'd always been influencing others: getting people on board with new ideas, persuading others to work in a different way. However, reaching out cold to corporate decision makers felt like climbing Mount Everest, out of reach, and the thought alone sent shivers down my spine.

I knew I had to find 'non-salesy' ways to open doors, using methods that drew on the skills I did have: getting into meaningful conversations, asking great questions and truly listening to what was being said. It was messy at first and a steep, sometimes nerve-racking, learning curve. Reaching out to people in my network who worked in corporates felt vulnerable. I wasn't asking for work but I was asking for feedback on my ideas and positioning. It still took courage. I worried they'd think I didn't know what I was doing (because honestly, at that stage, I didn't).

To my surprise, however, those conversations opened doors. One led to an opportunity to plan and facilitate a big event involving multiple public sector organisations. Another gave me the chance to coach leaders in a brand-new NHS service. Those early experiences gave me a much-needed boost. They didn't erase the self-doubt, but they helped to keep me going.

When I decided to expand beyond the public sector, I began attending local networking events. Most were

full of small business owners, many of them also trying to land bigger clients, just like me. I didn't find
corporate decision makers there, but I did get lucky.
Like many of us, I stumbled on a connection, someone who happened to be related to an HR director at
a well-known global company. We met, and because
I'd already done the work to clarify my positioning,
packages and pricing, we were able to co-create a
leadership development solution for his service leads
across the UK.

If you're hesitating to reach out to people in your network, I get it. It can feel exposing, like you're admitting
you don't have it all figured out, but those early conversations are where trust is built and clarity begins
to form. You don't need to have all the answers, just
the willingness to ask, listen and follow the thread of
what emerges. That's often where the real opportunities begin.

Those early wins gave me a taste of what was possible
and a growing belief that I could do this. Delivering
value, coaching leaders and seeing those light-bulb
moments felt incredible. Belief alone doesn't build
a business, however. Once those initial projects
wrapped up, I found myself back in the all-too-famil-
iar hustle, chasing the next lead, showing up to every
event, hoping another lucky connection might land.
That's when it hit me. I couldn't build something sustainable on chance and hope alone. I needed a proper

lead generation system that didn't rely on serendipity, but created consistent opportunities on purpose.

How my model was born

I started looking more closely at what the big consultancies were doing to win business. I'd worked with PricewaterhouseCoopers on a large public sector project, so I reached out to some old contacts – nervously, if I'm honest. People were generous with their time and their expertise. I learned about strategies like insight interviews and executive round tables, and realised something important. These weren't flashy sales tactics. They were built around thoughtful conversations and meaningful facilitation – skills I already had. Skills you have too. This is how the CSP began to take shape.

The key to both insights mining and executive round tables as strategies was finding a relevant hot topic and narrowing in on a specific industry or sector. Back in the early 2000s, without today's brilliant online tools, that took time. I remember trawling through trade journals, trying to get a sense of what mattered. Today, with AI and an overwhelming wealth of information at your fingertips, it's far easier to uncover what's going on. Speed doesn't replace empathy, however. You still need to fully listen, to tune in to what's keeping decision makers up at night and to understand their priorities through their lenses.

At the time, I decided to go big. I set out to interview twenty-five corporate decision makers, but by the time I reached the twelfth, I was hearing the same themes over and over. That's why I now suggest you keep it to between ten and twelve. It's more than enough to surface rich insights and start building momentum.

Off the back of those interviews, I hosted my first executive round table. I invited those who had taken part, plus a few other decision makers I was keen to connect with. Eight people showed up – and yes, this was all in person. No Zoom, no Teams; they didn't exist back then. Just a meeting room and a shared conversation. In the follow-up one-to-ones, I secured contracts, but more than that, I found a rhythm I genuinely enjoyed. It didn't feel salesy. It felt human.

Still, something didn't sit right. I realised I was making the process more complicated than it needed to be. I was using insight interviews to build the audience for the round table but I didn't need both. There was a simpler, more streamlined path. If you're just starting out, insight interviews are a brilliant way to build confidence, understand the language corporate clients use and uncover what really matters to them. Once you have that clarity, you can move straight into round tables. Trust yourself.

Even when you do everything right, know that things can go sideways. I remember one round table where only two people turned up. I was deflated. Embarrassed, even. I wanted to disappear into the floor but I chose to show up anyway. What followed was one of the richest conversations I've ever facilitated. In the one-to-one follow-ups, both attendees' organisations became clients. That experience taught me a lesson I've never forgotten: the size of the room doesn't determine the size of the opportunity.

Over time, I've continued to refine and adapt these strategies, especially in response to what's going on in the world. During the COVID-19 lockdowns, executive round tables took on new meaning. Corporate leaders were isolated, unsure and under pressure, craving connection and perspective. Facilitating those conversations established me not just as helpful, but as someone worth bringing in to work with them.

This approach hasn't worked only for me. Coaches, consultants and trainers I've supported have used these exact strategies to win meaningful, consistent corporate clients. You've already met a few of them in this book and there are more stories to come.

I hope that sharing the start of my journey encourages you to take imperfect action, because that's where momentum lives. Send that message, ask that question, book that meeting. One meaningful conversation will teach you more than a dozen planning sessions ever could. What happens if it doesn't go perfectly? That's OK. Every step forward gives you something towards clarity, confidence and insight. Remember: nothing is ever wasted.

You don't have to wait until you feel ready. You don't need to be perfect. If you're feeling unsure, overwhelmed or like there's just one more thing you need to figure out before you begin, you are not alone. That's exactly what we'll explore more deeply in the next section.

It's OK to ask for support

One of the biggest barriers I see for coaches, consultants and trainers moving into corporate work is the belief that they have to do it on their own. After all, many of us became solopreneurs to be independent, to prove we could go it alone, and in many ways, we have. That independent streak has likely served us well, as we've built our businesses through our resourcefulness, determination and care for our clients. When you're building something meaningful, especially something new, it's easy to slip into the habit of thinking you have to do it all yourself.

At a certain point, however, doing it all alone stops being efficient and starts being exhausting. You've figured out how to make things work, but stepping into consistent corporate work often calls for a new kind of approach – not just in strategy, but also in mindset. Corporate opportunities tend to unfold more slowly. The buying cycles are longer, the dynamics are different and the conversations take time. The change in pace can bring about uncomfortable doubts of *Am I doing this right? Why isn't this moving faster? Is it just me?* Add to that the mental load of delivering excellent work for your existing clients while also trying to break into new markets, and it's no wonder this part can feel heavier than expected. You're not alone in this, even if it sometimes feels like it.

Sometimes we're just too close to our businesses to see what's working and what's not. That's where a sounding board – a trusted peer, mentor or coach – becomes invaluable. Not because you're not capable, but because you're human. Because your perspective is limited when you're in the thick of it, and because talking it through often unlocks the clarity and momentum you've been trying to force on your own.

Support doesn't always need to be formal. It could look like:

- Asking a past client for feedback on your new positioning

- Reaching out to a contact in a corporate role for an insight interview

- Checking in with a peer who's navigating this same transition

It could also mean becoming part of a community where you don't have to explain yourself every time you share a win or a wobble. My Momentum community supports coaches, consultants and trainers who've been through the CSP and want to keep building, together. It's a space where you can stay focused, feel supported and be surrounded by others who understand both the highs and the hiccups of growing a corporate-facing business.

Whether it's Momentum or simply a trusted circle of peers, the message is the same: you weren't meant to do this alone. Get yourself into an environment that normalises the results you want in your business. You don't need to have it all figured out. You don't need to do it perfectly, and you definitely don't need to carry the whole load yourself.

This next phase of your business isn't just about scaling or signing more clients – it's about doing those things in a way that feels right, grounded and supported. When you stop trying to hold everything yourself, you make more space for creativity, for energy and for meaningful connection with the people who can help you grow. Take the next step with someone by your side. You might be surprised how much lighter it feels and how much faster things start to move.

Now that you're giving yourself permission to be supported, let's turn to something just as liberating: you don't have to start from scratch. You already have strengths, strategies and assets that are working. In the next chapter, we'll explore how to recognise them, adapt them and use them to win corporate clients with more ease and confidence.

12
Use What Works Now

When you're stepping into something new, like consistently working with corporate clients, it's easy to feel like you need to reinvent yourself. Maybe you've been wondering whether your experience still counts, whether you need a different brand or whether you have to grasp a whole new set of skills before you're ready. Let's pause that thought right here. You already have more than enough to get started.

This chapter is about recognising and reclaiming what's already working in your business. It's about building on the strengths, tools and approaches you've developed over years of coaching, consulting or training and learning how to adapt them to work brilliantly in the corporate space. You don't need to start from scratch. You just need to start where you are.

Before we look at what to do next, let's look at what's already in your hands:

- Your ability to listen deeply and ask powerful questions

- Your signature frameworks or workshop content

- The transformations you've helped individuals or teams create

- The testimonials, case studies and results you've gathered

- Your experience working across different industries or cultures

- Your relationships with clients, peers and former colleagues

These aren't just things you've done. They're assets. When articulated clearly, they become part of your value proposition, the answer to the 'why you?' that corporate decision makers are quietly scanning for. This isn't about reinvention, it's about translation. You're reframing your experience in a way that speaks directly to what matters in the corporate context.

If you've already worked with a few corporate clients, start there and look at what went well by answering the following questions:

- What were the themes that resonated?

- What kind of people championed your work internally?

- What language did they use when talking about the value you brought?

My corporate client leaders often talk about the clarity and confidence they have gained, better collaboration in their teams, the ability to delegate more effectively and be more strategic, and the improvements in resolving conflict, demonstrating more agility and adaptability. I'm sure you have a similar list, which will give you insights into how your value is perceived by corporate decision makers.

If you've worked mostly with smaller businesses or individuals, don't discount that experience either. Look at the problems you've helped solve and ask yourself where these same challenges show up in the corporate world, because they do. You don't need to build a whole new offer if the one you already have just needs a slight reframe. For example, think how the coaching approach you've used with private individuals could be packaged for senior leaders who are trying to realign their teams during major change.

You don't have to lose yourself

One of the most common concerns I hear from coaches, consultants and trainers is 'Will I have to change who I am to work with corporates?' It's a real fear. Many of us have built our businesses around who we are – our style, our creativity, our methods – and the idea of becoming more 'corporate' can feel like trading in your soul for sensible shoes and a set of bullet points. You don't have to lose yourself to work with corporates, but you do need to learn how to translate your brilliance into language and formats that corporate decision makers understand and value.

Corporates aren't looking for watered-down versions of what you do. They're not asking for generic solutions. In fact, many of them are drowning in generic. What they want is something that works, something human, relevant and credible. That often means bringing in people who understand people. People like you.

Take Simon Hawtrey-Woore, founder of The Outspire and a client of mine. He specialises in coaching senior leaders to step out of the noise and see the bigger picture. Simon's sessions aren't run in boardrooms – they're held outdoors. He quite literally takes leaders outside to 'outspire' them. It's a human approach to a familiar corporate challenge of strategic thinking and perspective, and it works, because it's delivered with clarity, purpose and confidence.

Then there's Clara Heimerdinger, founder of Nice 'N' Spikey Comedy, another client of mine. She brings teams together through an event she calls Comedy in the Office. It's playful, smart and deeply bonding for teams who are often stuck in cycles of pressure and formality. On paper, it might sound too quirky, but in practice, it's exactly the kind of energising, morale-boosting solution that organisations need more of. Clara's offering is far from generic and it's aligned to real business challenges.

Then there's Linda (not her real name). Linda designs and delivers leadership development programmes. She had her eye on a particular organisation she wanted to work with, but her outreach to the CEO had gone unanswered. Twice. I read the message she'd sent and saw that it was perfectly professional... but a little too safe. A little too generic. I encouraged her to write from the heart and say clearly why she felt inspired to work with that organisation. She did, and she got a reply that same day. This led to a meeting, and then a corporate contract. The difference? She showed up as herself, with conviction.

You don't need to be loud, high-energy or extroverted to succeed in the corporate space. That's not me either. Some of the most effective corporate coaches, consultants and trainers I know are thoughtful, quietly confident and deeply curious.

If there's only one thing you take from this chapter, it should be this: you don't need to become someone else to work with corporates. You just need to speak their language while still being fluent in your own. You're not trying to blend in. You're trying to stand out for all the right reasons. Corporate decision makers are looking for people who can help them move the needle and do it in a way that connects with their people. That's what you bring. You don't need to leave your creativity, your story or your style at the door. You just need to package it with clarity and confidence – and that's something you already know how to do.

You don't need a perfect plan, a brand overhaul or a whole new identity. You already have the foundations, so what's needed now is the courage to build on them. Start where the traction is. Use the stories, tools and experiences that already resonate. Reframe them, test them, talk about them. Momentum builds through action, not endless behind-the-scenes preparation.

It's reassuring to realise you don't need to reinvent the wheel. Much of what's working for you now can be amplified but, to turn those occasional wins into your norm, there's a deeper shift required – and it starts with how you see yourself.

13
Becoming The Person Your Next Client Is Looking For

There comes a point in any business journey where you realise it's not about more strategies and better tactics – it's about how you see yourself and about the powerful beliefs that shape the decisions you make, the opportunities you pursue and the way you carry yourself in conversations. This chapter is about stepping into the version of you who fully owns your value.

This is about identity, not competence, and it shapes every result you get, even the ones you can't explain. Think back to the last time something clicked in your business. A moment when a corporate decision maker responded positively to your outreach, or a proposal landed easily without you needing to justify your pricing, or you stood in front of a room centred in your expertise.

If you trace those moments back you'll probably notice a shift in how you showed up. It wasn't about having the perfect words – it was about how you felt about yourself. The ease of your tone, the comfort in your expertise and the clarity with which you spoke about your value – that's identity at work.

The identity you carry is often invisible but it shows up everywhere. It runs through every interaction from how you write your LinkedIn posts to how you open conversations and how you handle discussions around pricing and budget. People can sense it.

It plays out in how quickly you reach out to decision makers, how comfortable you are holding space with senior leaders and whether you instinctively put yourself forward to larger opportunities or shy away from them. You can have world-class skills and expertise and still shrink in these moments if your identity hasn't shifted. Equally, you can be imperfect and learning and still land great clients because you carry yourself as someone worth listening to.

One of the most frustrating things I see is capable, experienced coaches, consultants and trainers unconsciously settling into an identity that keeps them playing small. Often, it's an identity shaped by beliefs like 'I'm great at delivery, but I'm not naturally good at business development,' or 'I know others charge far more for work that isn't as strong as mine, but something still holds me back from raising my rates that high.' The stories we tell ourselves get repeated quietly in our heads, in how we market ourselves and even in how we price. Over time they can shape our business in ways that make it feel like we've hit a ceiling, but the ceilings are usually self-imposed and identity is where we start to break through them.

Trusted partners don't wait to be chosen

One of the habits I've seen time and again is playing the waiting game: waiting for someone to notice them, waiting for a lucky introduction and waiting for someone else to validate that they belong in the room. It's a habit that can feel comfortable, especially if you are used to work arriving through referrals.

The most impactful businesses I know are not built on waiting. They are built on choosing. Choosing to show up where decisions are made, choosing to initiate conversations that lead to meaningful work, and choosing to lead with clarity about how you help organisations thrive.

Trusted partners are not granted permission. They claim space through consistent, value-driven action. A brilliant example of this comes from Mark (not his real name), one of the coaches I've worked with. Like you, Mark already had strong expertise. People liked him and they knew that he was good at what he did, but his corporate opportunities were sporadic. He found himself wondering, *How do I get taken seriously by bigger organisations?*

One of the biggest shifts Mark experienced was through how he started showing up by taking action that aligned with the identity of a trusted partner. He chose to lead insight interviews, running executive round tables, be in the room as a peer to decision makers rather than a supplier trying to get booked.

One of Mark's existing contacts, someone who had known him for years, saw him differently after experiencing him in action during a round-table discussion. That person later told Mark they had known what he did but they hadn't really seen the depth of value he could bring until they witnessed how he facilitated conversations with decision makers. Soon after, Mark was brought into that organisation on a tangible contract – all because he showed up differently and people responded to the more confident version of him they saw in the room.

Every coach, consultant or trainer I know who thrives in the corporate space made the identity shift before the big names appeared on their website or the steady pipeline of contracts formed. This is the quiet power of deciding you belong.

This shift often doesn't feel dramatic. There's no big fanfare or immediate rush of new clients. What you will notice is a quiet sense of resolve and a calmer confidence when you talk about your work, and people respond to that energy. You become the person your next client is looking for by choosing to own the identity you've been growing into all along.

You'll start seeing it reflected back in conversations that feel warmer and more open, and opportunities that feel less like lucky breaks and more like natural steps. The work itself becomes more enjoyable because you are collaborating at a deeper, more strategic level.

We've covered a lot of ground and you probably have a list of actions. There's no pressure to do it all today but you do have to make a quiet, firm decision: are you someone who brings value at the highest level, who helps organisations solve meaningful problems? Are you someone who belongs in these conversations and are you ready to show up in a way that reflects that?

There's no rush but you do have to decide because from this decision, everything else starts to shift.

This chapter is your internal pivot point. The person you need to become to enjoy a simpler, more consistent, more commercially valuable business is already within you. Now it's about choosing to make that version of you your new default. Your future clients are ready for you to show up in this way.

This is your permission slip, if you need it, to stop playing small, to step fully into your value and build a business that reflects the leader you are becoming. Everything else in this pathway will work even better when it's aligned with this version of you. Let's step into it fully and on your own terms.

Now let's talk about what you can look forward to.

The rewards ahead

Right now, you might be feeling a little daunted by the thought of the time and patience it takes to build traction with corporate clients, especially if you're used to private clients and small business owners moving quickly, giving instant feedback and signing off without committee approval. Corporate work moves differently – it is slower, more layered and, at times, less certain – but what's on the other side of that effort is, as well as more work, more impact, more meaning and more freedom.

I won't pretend this is a magic bullet. Building meaningful, sustainable work takes intention, patience and persistence but it doesn't have to take forever. Many of my coach, consultant and trainer clients have experienced their first wins within weeks, whether that's a key conversation opening up, a renewed sense of clarity or early client engagements. The bigger wins, like consistent high-value clients and greater ease in your business, build over months not years. The more you put in upfront, the more it pays off in freedom, confidence and predictable revenue.

Let me introduce you to a few people who've already walked this path. Not one of them started with it all figured out; in fact, many of them began where you might be right now – full of capability and drive, but hesitant on the steps. These aren't polished success stories. They're real people who met their doubts, showed up consistently and created a business that works on their terms.

Jeanette Forder: From one-off sessions to confident, long-term partnerships with corporates

Jeanette is a highly skilled coach with a deep commitment to supporting women through menopause, but like many mission-driven professionals, she found herself stuck when it came to securing consistent corporate work. She had managed the occasional one-off session in a corporate setting but struggled to turn interest into ongoing opportunities.

Business development overwhelmed her. Reaching out made her feel like she was selling herself. She cared deeply, but didn't know how to bridge the gap between her values and the structured world of corporates. She wanted to show up using her authentic voice, one that expressed her spirituality and a deeply human approach, but worried that it wouldn't be taken seriously in a corporate environment.

During our work together, Jeanette experienced a shift not just in strategy, but in how she saw herself. She found a way to show up in the corporate space without compromising her values. That meant, using her words, moving from 'please work with me' energy to 'If we're aligned, let's explore what's possible.'

She discovered that business development didn't have to feel forced. She began showing up with clarity and confidence, creating conversations that felt like genuine relationship-building, not like she was performing.

Jeanette now:

- Works just three days a week while earning more than before

- Has doubled her revenue

- Brings in aligned clients through genuine conversations – not cold tactics

Jeanette didn't compromise who she was to succeed in the corporate space, she clarified it, owned it and built a business around it.

Paul Grainger: From uncertainty to clarity, confidence and corporate success

When Paul embarked on the CSP, he was in transition. After years in education, he was starting a new chapter but wasn't sure what it would look like. He didn't have a clear offer, he wasn't sure who to speak to, and the idea of selling into corporates felt overwhelming.

At the start, Paul didn't just lack a roadmap, he lacked belief, although he didn't recognise it at the time. The corporate world felt like something 'other', something for people with more business experience or more polish, and yet he knew he had something valuable to offer.

Through the CSP, Paul developed a clear signature programme and a practical structure for engaging with decision makers. He ran a series of insight interviews that gave him a deeper understanding of the challenges his target clients were facing. From there, he launched a series of executive round tables that not only elevated his visibility, but helped him be seen as a credible partner in the leadership development space.

Some of the attendees were already in his network, but hadn't taken him seriously until they experienced his facilitation first-hand. One round table led directly to an invitation to submit a proposal and opened the door to new conversations and more paid work.

Now Paul:

- Is delivering leadership development programmes for several corporate clients

- Runs regular executive round tables to stay visible and build trust

- Speaks on conference stages and brings his experience to wider audiences

- Has built a business that reflects both his values and his capability

The most profound shift for Paul wasn't just in results, it was in identity. He no longer wonders if he can do this. Now he knows he can.

Christine Michaelis: From scattered services to focused corporate work delivered with confidence

Christine had already built a business. For over a decade, she had supported entrepreneurs and start-ups, but she felt drawn to the corporate world and unsure how to enter it. Her knowledge was deep, but her business development felt haphazard. She knew she had something valuable; she just didn't know how to translate it into a consistent, compelling offer for corporate clients.

Through our work together, Christine clarified her specialism: helping leaders and teams communicate more effectively. She moved country and felt like she was starting over again, but by building a consistent strategy using insight interviews and executive round tables, she quickly had corporate wins.

Within weeks, Christine was:

- Meeting the right decision makers

- Hosting executive round tables with corporate leaders

- Receiving invitations to submit proposals

- Securing longer-term engagements including team training and executive coaching

Christine no longer feels scattered. She is focused, strategic and in demand. She has built relationships that go far beyond a single workshop.

Simon Hawtrey-Woore: From ad hoc clients to aligned, confident growth in the corporate space

Simon had had some success with corporate clients before we worked together, but business development felt inconsistent and energy-draining. He was confident in his coaching but less so in how to create a repeatable, aligned way of securing work. He joined the CSP thinking he'd tidy up his operations, but what he got was far deeper.

Simon found new clarity in his offers and more confidence in how he engaged with decision makers. Instead of pitching, he began having conversations that were grounded, intentional and relaxed.

Since then, Simon has:

- Attracted strong referrals

- Become a trusted partner to his many corporate clients

- Grown his business in a way that feels human and sustainable

He's no longer viewing meetings as pressure-filled moments, but as genuine conversations rooted in value and listening. That shift alone has opened new doors and made the business development process feel more natural and effective. The real win for Simon wasn't just more clients. It was finally building a business that reflected his values and his voice.

Each of these stories is different, but each person started with uncertainty about how to make things work in a new context. Now they are doing it. Not perfectly, but meaningfully, sustainably and in ways that feel true to who they are. This is what's possible: more impact, more freedom and more connection with work that feels truly worthwhile for you.

Conclusion: The Power Of A Clear Pathway

In this book, we have been laying the foundation for achieving long-term, trusted success with corporate clients in a way that doesn't feel salesy. Having a clear, structured pathway like this matters, because when you're no longer guessing what to do next, everything changes.

You've explored the five strategic steps that make up the CSP: Position, Package, Price, Prospect and Promote. Together they form the essential building blocks of winning corporate clients in a way that is intentional, consistent and aligned with who you are. This isn't about aggressive tactics, flashy branding or chasing after organisations hoping they'll notice you. It's about owning your expertise, solving business challenges and building meaningful relationships with decision makers based on trust.

Having worked through the CSP, you now have the map, so let's make sure you're using it to best effect. This is the perfect time to reflect and get honest with yourself on where you are already strong and where you are hesitating, second-guessing or feeling underprepared.

You've also had a go at completing my Corporate Success Scorecard, a quick online tool that gives you a snapshot of your current strengths and areas for growth across all five steps to help you get a clear sense of where you stand. This is a great time to look at it again to see what improvements you've already made by working through the tasks associated with each step here in this book.

If you haven't already completed it, try it now.

Take the scorecard here:

https://corporatesuccess.scoreapp.com.

You'll receive your results instantly along with personalised suggestions for ways to focus your time, energy and actions on the areas that will make the biggest difference.

The CSP gives you structure, direction and clarity, but if you're anything like the many coaches and consultants I've worked with, you might also feel the stirrings of self-doubt right now. You might be thinking: *I love this but where do I even begin?*, *What if I do all this work and still get ignored?* or *I'm not sure I'm 'corporate' enough to even pull this off.*

This isn't a strategy issue; this is about the inner resistance that shows up when you're stretching into something bigger. If you don't acknowledge this now, it will quietly run the show. That's why in Part Three we turned our attention inward to explore the real inhibitors of change, the ones that live inside us, because long-term success with corporate clients isn't just about what you do – it's also about what you believe and, more importantly, what you believe you are capable of.

Momentum in action

There's a beautiful shift that happens when things start to click, and it's not some magical force that just appears one day – it's the result of small, thoughtful actions done consistently and strategically. Once it starts, it changes everything. Now it's time for you to bring the concept of momentum to life by knowing what it looks like, how it feels and how to keep it going, especially in a space like corporate work, where the rewards build over time.

Momentum often starts quietly. A decision maker replies to your message and wants to talk. A follow-up conversation with someone from your executive round table turns into an enthusiastic exchange about what a solution could look like. Someone loops you into a three-way message saying they need to speak to you as someone who understands how to work with their challenge. Each of these is a sign that your positioning is resonating, your promotion strategies are working and your presence is starting to stick. It's proof that the seeds you've planted are beginning to grow.

One of the most satisfying things about momentum is that it feeds your confidence in a grounded, quiet sense, which comes across to corporate decision makers as you knowing what you're doing. It starts with trusting yourself in conversations, speaking more clearly about your value, saying no to work that doesn't fit and holding your pricing with calm conviction. That confidence creates more opportunities. It's magnetic and quietly compelling to the right people. This is often the point where corporate clients begin to find you.

The key to sustaining momentum is consistency, not intensity. You don't have to sprint, you just have to keep moving. Keep nurturing your existing relationships. Keep reaching out with insights and creating rooms to meet decision makers. Keep refining your message based on what's landing. Keep showing up in ways that feel true to you. You'll find that some of the strategies, like insight interviews, round tables or following up on a warm lead, become even more effective once you've got some traction. The more you build momentum, the less you need to push. Your work starts to speak for itself. Your name comes up in the right rooms. You start to shape your business around the kind of work, and the kind of life, you want.

Momentum isn't magic, it's movement: a series of imperfect actions, refined over time, that turn into something powerful. You don't need to do everything perfectly – you just need to keep showing up with clarity, relevance and connection. The rest will unfold.

You didn't come this far just to keep juggling clients or patching together short-term projects. You've built too much experience for that. You're here because you know there's a better way, work that's more consistent, more valuable and more satisfying. Momentum is the sign that you're moving towards that steadier, more fulfilling business. The clarity you've found, the conversations you've had, the shifts you've made – they all count. From here, your next steps don't need to be giant leaps, just intentional ones. As we come to the end of the book, I want to leave you with an idea that is simple, but important: you are closer than you think, you have done more than you realise, and you don't have to do any of it alone.

Let's wrap this together. One final message, just for you.

You are unique

If you've made it this far, you are already different. You are not just interested in corporate work but are ready to engage fully with it. Not one day, not when everything is perfectly aligned, but now, in your own way and with your own voice. Remember: this pathway is about bringing the best of who you are into spaces that need exactly that. Yes, it takes courage, but if you have read this far, you already have it.

I know what it's like to be in your shoes. This isn't some academic exercise for me. For more than twenty years I have worked with corporates, not just selling into them but delivering leadership and transformational programmes across regions, industries and cultures. I know how much energy it takes to keep showing up and delivering excellent work while still wondering where the next opportunity is coming from.

This book is not about turning you into a salesperson. It's about helping you engage the right corporate decision makers and get paid properly and consistently for the difference you already know how to make.

You don't need to water down what you do, you don't need to wait to be discovered and you definitely don't need to become someone else. You simply need to apply a clear pathway, backed by structure, strategy and a bit of courage to bring the work you care about into the rooms where it matters most.

You've got this. Now go make it real.

The CSP Programme

B y now, you've seen what's possible. You've read true stories, gathered insight, maybe even recognised parts of yourself in these journeys, but here's the truth: information isn't the hard part anymore. The hard part is implementation – turning what you now know into something you do, consistently. Turning ideas into action and action into income.

That's why I created the CSP Programme – a practical, supportive space to help you bridge the gap between your expertise and consistent, well-paid corporate work. This shift isn't just strategic, it's personal. It's about stepping into a bigger version of what's already within you and doing it in a way that feels aligned, supported and doable. At the heart of the programme is the CSP you've been learning throughout this book,

but we go beyond that with a full business development framework to build consistency and flow.

Yes, you'll get strategies, learn how to position yourself so corporates get what you offer, how to package
your services, how to confidently price and how to
attract the right decision makers. That's all in there
as the five steps of the CSP. More importantly, however, you'll start to believe and see you can do this.
You'll build momentum. You'll stop spinning. You'll
stop hiding behind 'just one more tweak'. You'll start
making progress and feel proud of it. You'll go from
wondering if consistent corporate clients are possible
for you to having a practical plan to reach out to them
and seeing multiple opportunities unfold.

You'll learn about:

- Transitioning smoothly from sharing insights to
  selling your packages

- Thought leadership that builds your credibility
  over time

- Simple systems for nurturing and following up

- Practical ways to grow without burning out or
  compromising who you are

You'll receive support in the form of:

- Group coaching so you can apply what you're
  learning in real time

- Accountability calls to keep your momentum going

- Self-paced online modules to revisit whenever you need

- Templates, swipe copy and tools that save hours of second-guessing

- Personal feedback and support from me – I'm in this with you

- A WhatsApp community of like-minded peers so you're never doing this alone

You followed Jeanette's story in earlier chapters, so let me share with you what she said about the programme:

'Before this year, I was scrabbling around working with anybody and everybody. Now, I've grown into a different space where I don't need to be somebody else. I've held boundaries, embraced my truth, and found a new level of authenticity in how I work with clients. I've had my best quarter ever, doubled my revenue for the year, and shifted from casual chats into proper sales conversations that convert. The unexpected part? The personal growth. I came in expecting a process, and I got that – but I also walked away with clarity, confidence, and a business that now fits with the life I actually want.'

—Jeanette Forder, founder of
Phoenix Wellness

Let me hold out an invitation: if you're ready to stop second-guessing yourself and start showing up with clarity and confidence in the corporate space, the CSP Programme is here to support you. You don't have to go on this journey alone, and you don't have to wait until you feel 'ready'.

Check out the full programme details here: www.corporatesuccesspathway.com/prog.

Next steps

The following resources will support you in getting consistent corporate clients (some are paid and some are free).

The Corporate Success Scorecard

This is a free, practical starting point if you're not sure where to focus your energy first. There is a series of questions that score you on the five key elements of the CSP outlined in this book, giving you a clear, honest picture of where you're strong and where you could level up. You'll receive a personalised score across each area, along with a customised report that highlights quick wins and longer-term opportunities.

Visit: https://corporatesuccess.scoreapp.com.

Corporate Opportunities Webinar

A free webinar held on a regular basis throughout the year updating you on what's going on in the corporate world and where the opportunities lie for you.

Visit: www.corporateopportunities.info

The CSP Programme

Our flagship programme for coaches, consultants and trainers who want to consistently win corporate clients without compromising their values.

Visit: www.corporatesuccesspathway.com/prog.

References

1 International Coach Federation, *2016 ICT Global Coaching Study: Executive Summary* (2016), https://coachingfederation.org/app/uploa ds/2017/12/2016ICFGlobalCoachingStudy_ ExecutiveSummary-2.pdf, accessed 23 June 2025

2 R Waite, *The Coaching Industry Report 2025* (2025), www.robinwaite.com/coaching-industry-report, accessed 23 June 2025

3 R Bohne, 'Consulting industry worldwide – statistics & facts' (Statista, 2024), www.statista. com/topics/8112/global-consulting-services-industry/, accessed 23 June 2025

4 J Hurley, 'UK consulting industry to grow again after year of contraction', *The Times* (10 March 2025), www.thetimes.com/ business-money/companies/article/uk-

consulting-industry-to-grow-again-after-year-of-contraction-m9zt9kj3t?utm, accessed 22 July 2025

5   Association for Talent Development, 'ATD Research: L&D Professionals Are Optimistic About TD's Value Within Organizations' (2024), www.td.org/content/press-release/atd-research-l-and-d-professionals-are-optimistic-about-td-s-value-within-organizations, accessed 23 June 2025

6   Gartner, *Top 5 HR Trends and Priorities That Matter Most in 2025* (2025), www.gartner.com/en/human-resources/trends/top-priorities-for-hr-leaders, accessed 23 June 2025

7   K Dewar, 'Top 20 HR challenges in 2025 and how to solve them' (Achievers, 2025), www.achievers.com/blog/hr-challenges/, accessed 23 June 2025

8   DDI, *Global Leadership Forecast 2025* (2025), www.ddiworld.com/research/global-leadership-forecast-2025, accessed 23 June 2025

9   T Jadar, 'The Real Costs Of Employee Turnover In 2025' (Applauz, 2025), www.applauz.me/resources/costs-of-employee-turnover, accessed 23 June 2025

10   J Harter, 'U.S. Employee Engagement Sinks to 10-Year Low' (Gallup, 2025), www.gallup.com/workplace/654911/employee-engagement-sinks-year-low.aspx, accessed 23 June 2025

11   M Martinez et al, 'The Health and Economic Burden of Employee Burnout to U.S.

Employers', *American Journal of Preventative Medicine*, 68/4 (April 2025), pp.645–655, www.ajpmonline.org/article/S0749-3797(25)00023-6/abstract, accessed 23 June 2025

12 J Garcia, 'Common pitfalls in transformations: A conversation with Jon Garcia' (McKinsey Transformation, 29 March 2022), www.mckinsey.com/capabilities/transformation/our-insights/common-pitfalls-in-transformations-a-conversation-with-jon-garcia, accessed 23 June 2025

13 M Michalowicz, *Profit First: Transform Your Business from a Cash-Eating Monster to a Money-Making Machine* (Portfolio/Penguin, 2017)

14 M Pratt, 'Coaching Statistics: The ROI of Coaching in 2024' (International Coaching Federation, 2024), https://coachingfederation.org/blog/coaching-statistics-the-roi-of-coaching-in-2024, accessed 23 June 2025

15 Intellek, 'Measure Corporate Training ROI' (no date), https://intellek.io/blog/measure-corporate-training-roi, accessed 23 June 2025

Acknowledgements

This book wouldn't exist without the people who've shaped my thinking and encouraged me to keep going.

To my incredible clients; you've been my greatest teachers. The insights, stories and results you've shared have brought this book to life far more than any theory could. I'm especially grateful to Paul Grainger, Christine Michaelis, Simon Hawtrey-Woore and Jeanette Forder for allowing me to share glimpses of your journeys; your progress and reflections have been inspiring to witness.

A big thank you to Ashley Libby Diaz and Joel Young. Your generosity in listening, sense-checking and sharing honest reflections has meant more than you probably realise. I've appreciated every conversation and idea bounced along the way.

To everyone who's cheered me on, challenged my thinking, or simply asked, '*How's the book coming along?*', thank you. It's kept me moving.

And finally, to you, the person holding this book. I hope it serves as a reminder that you don't need to overcomplicate things to create a fulfilling, commercially successful business. You already have more than enough within you to build something that works. This is just the nudge to help you do it.

The Author

Nicky has spent the last twenty years helping leaders thrive in complex, multicultural organisations and, more recently, supporting coaches and consultants to win meaningful work with corporate clients in a way that feels natural, ethical and commercially sound.

She is the founder and CEO of WAVA Global, a leadership development company that has worked in twenty-eight countries with a wide range of organisations, from global household names to ambitious regional players. She is also the creator of the Corporate Success Pathway, a structured and proven pathway for building a successful B2B business, along with the CSP Programme, and Momentum, a membership community that supports implementation.

With a background in psychology, service improvement and transformation, Nicky is driven by helping people lead with clarity, empathy and impact. She believes business should support a fulfilling life and not consume it. For her, that includes the freedom to travel, explore and work with clients around the world.

She's known for showing people how to be taken seriously in the corporate world without having to force it, fake it or become someone they're not. It's not about being louder or more polished – it's about being clear, thoughtful and deeply credible in a way that's true to who you are. In her CSP, Nicky has built a clear, human and strategic approach to building a business that reflects who you are and opens doors you might not have thought possible, and it is an approach she has seen work time and again.

⊕ www.corporatesuccesspathway.com

🅵 www.facebook.com/nicky.davies.7359

🅸🅽 www.linkedin.com/in/
   nicky-j-davies-executivecoach